Vagish Naganur is a graduate in architecture and a postgraduate in landscape design from CEPT, Ahmedabad. He moved from this dry city to Bengaluru, the city of more than just gardens. With his fondness for wilderness and his desire for emptiness, his interests branched out further by intertwining with many firms as their consultant and as design faculty with a few schools of architecture. He loves treading the informal path, unravelling hidden stories along its trail and now, with this budding foray into storytelling, is trying to live up to his name fame, *Vagish:* The God of speech.

Gurjit Singh Matharoo was conferred an International Fellow of the Royal Institute of British Architects in 2012 - only the third Indian, after architects B.V.Doshi and Charles Correa, to receive this honour. The studio, Matharoo Associates, has gained international and domestic acclaim for their innovative work and are winners of the 2011 Chicago Athenaeum Architectural Award, the 2010 AR House Award and the 2009 Emerging Architecture Award, to name a few. Gurjit enjoys teaching and was visiting faculty from 1991-2016 and the Chair of architectural design from 2016-2019 at his alma mater CEPT, Ahmedabad. He is deeply passionate about all things mechanical and is often seen riding his naked Ducati to work.

'This book from two architects promises a plan that will leave you contemplating the blueprint of life. A bumpy journey through moral dilemmas, fearless decisions, uncertain irony in what is a snappy, quick and telling collection and I daresay, make for some clever reading. Crown it all with the ability to laugh at themselves.

Enjoy! Albeit, in a truly joyous and effervescent manner. The way things unfold and above all, the combination of intellect and lightness of being, mostly going hand in glove, create an easy atmosphere. You could look for a moral at the end of each story and mostly find the one that concludes the uncertain aspects of life.'
Rocky. TV Anchor, Food Professional, Author

'What started with commissions from *Wallpaper* and *Architectural Review* to shoot Gurjit's works since 2008 has ended up in a strong bond over photographic *jugaads* and afternoon naps. Being kidnapped by him is always fun, he reminiscing while me looking through the lens. The book is loaded with amusing insights into 'Matharoo world' with a peek into his creative process. It also reminds me why we are both friends beyond profession.'
Edmund Sumner. Architectural Photographer, Author

'Sometimes, you feel a spontaneous gratitude for living at the same time as some creators of immense beauty. My giddy gushings while watching (Shane) Warne's balls of geometric improbabilities, (Anupam) Sud's tempestuous artwork, and (Leonard) Cohen's singing *Hallelujah*, seem to sketch my own inner perturbances. I felt that same rare wave of fulfillment crash into my dried, shrivelled heart. An account of the inner workings of a master, a gift we mustn't take casually. I affirm to the universe, I'd been dazzled.'
Rabbi Shergill. Urban Balladeer

'Karma and reincarnation have the most extraordinary ways of returning. Brimming with intrigue and magical narratives, this thread of anecdotal tales will delight, amuse and stimulate those brave enough to tread the twisted paths, which may seem inevitable but offer mystique and surprise at every turn.

The book is beautifully conceived, compelling reading and so much more than it 'says on the tin.' I realised with a smile that each and every story has snippets of their remarkable journey, of hand-holding, tears and satisfied hurrahs, all sandwiched together with delicious tales of the need-to-tread-gently with clients, gurus, dogs and masterji's.

There are many beauties to the prose, the immediate one being the easy and fluid writing style, littered with wit, which engages the reader from the first line. Easily relatable to all, and the footnotes are particularly useful. Beguiling and dazzling in so many ways. Five stories and four chillies in, I was hooked.'
Laura Williams. Curator, Author, South-Asian Art Advisor - 18th to 21st Century, Owner of Art 18|21

'Sen always said that as an Oncologist although I have a great sense of tumour, I have no sense of humour. During these difficult times of his failing health, I have been reading out stories to him and laughing my heart out, leaving him amused and happy. This witty book came as a delightful way to look at life. Very therapeutic.'
Dr. Asha Kapadia. Oncologist
Sen Kapadia. Architect

WIT·NESS TO MAT·HAROO
(मत हारो / *never give up*)
SPIRIT

Short stories based
on true life events

Gurjit Singh Matharoo and
'Sutradhar' Vagish Naganur

ORO
EDITIONS

EDITIONS

Publishers of Architecture, Art, and Design
Gordon Goff: Publisher

www.oroeditions.com
info@oroeditions.com

Published by ORO Editions

Graphic Design: Anisha Chacko
Text: Gurjit Singh Matharoo and Vagish Naganur
Matharoo Associates Editor: Trisha Patel
ORO Managing Editor: Kirby Anderson

10 9 8 7 6 5 4 3 2 1 First Edition

Library of Congress data available upon request. World Rights: Available

ISBN: 978-1-961856-46-2

Color Separations and Printing: ORO Editions, Inc.
Printed in China.

International Distribution: www.oroeditions.com/distribution

ORO Editions makes a continuous effort to minimize the overall carbon
footprint of its publications. As part of this goal, ORO Editions, in association
with Global ReLeaf, arranges to plant trees to replace those used in the
manufacturing of the paper produced for its books. Global ReLeaf is an
international campaign run by American Forests, one of the world's oldest
nonprofit conservation organizations. Global ReLeaf is American Forests'
education and action program that helps individuals, organizations, agencies,
and corporations improve the local and global environment by planting and
caring for trees.

To Papaji,

who burdened G enough so his
legs wouldn't tremble

+ *Refer to the story, 'Loaded Donkey and the Flying Carpet,' page 169*

Contents

Foreword: V.Raghunathan

For decades, my encounters with architecture were limited to interactions with friends in the field or through the lens of being a client myself. I harboured the perhaps mistaken belief that architects prioritised their creativity and design aesthetics over the needs, comfort and convenience of their clients. It was through perusing this delightful book that I found gratification in discovering that architects face their own trials and tribulations in dealing with their creative pursuits. *Wit-ness to Mat-Haroo Spirit* is a series of charmingly written stories by architects Gurjit Singh Matharoo and Vagish Naganur that shed light on the nuanced relationships and challenges architects contend with. These anecdotes span a 30-year career, providing a fascinating insight into the inner workings of an acclaimed practice - an uncharted territory thus far in architectural writing. Filled with self-deprecating humour in its folds, it gives us a quirky look into the special place the profession occupies, going beyond mere physical edifices to symbolise culture, history and human connections. Within the realm of literature, this quaint and engaging prose invites readers on a distinctive voyage, unravelling the complexities of architectural existence.

Some episodes take us to the vibrant city of Ahmedabad, where the young architects of this book grapple with the balancing act of design dilemmas, demands and budgets, as well as the whims of fate amidst romantic pursuits and tragedies. To me personally, the tales strike a chord, particularly resonating with my two decades of living not far from the renowned institute CEPT (Centre for Environment Planning and Technology), the crucible where the authors honed their architectural skills. Vagish also shares my adopted city of settling down, Bengaluru. I welcome readers to immerse themselves in these stimulating snippets, a testament to their rich experiences as freelance architects. We witness, albeit with 'wit,' the poignant struggles of architects striving to bring their grand visions to life, only to face setbacks and the unforgiving passage of time.

The narratives reveal the dreams, aspirations and emotional depth that shape the lives of the passionate architects, as they navigate through intricacies of their guild and fathom the true essence of success and fulfilment in a world that often prioritises profits over artistic integrity. The stories delve into themes of love, loss and the transient nature of human existence, etched deep into the pages of this book.

Here, architecture extends beyond mere construction and materials; it reflects society and its paradoxes, showcases human creativity and fallacies, while exhibiting unyielding resilience and the power of storytelling. This anthology mirrors the diverse tapestry of architectural wonders, from sprawling campuses to humble abodes, from crematoriums to blood banks, modern marvels to weathered ruins, teleporting readers into an almost mystical land, weaving enchanting tales along the way.

Each structure harbours a story waiting to be unearthed, intertwined with the lives of those who inhabit them, often leading to comical scenarios. The layered meanings, strange coincidences and bizarre endings are what make some of them sound truly unbelievable.

Embark on this literary voyage through the eyes and hearts of the blue-blooded architects, where architecture transcends being a mere backdrop and emerges as a character, shaping lives, loves and destinies of those within its embrace. It becomes a vessel of inspiration and solace, leaving lasting imprints on those it touches with its gamut of human emotions. The book stands as a tribute to the transformative power of architecture, encapsulating realms of innovation and beauty with madness!

It is precisely these wider interests that make this book for a readership way beyond the domain of architects alone, its affable language filled with puns and alliterations, adding to its universal appeal. Let the words transport you to a world where buildings breathe, walls whisper and windows unveil infinite possibilities.

Enjoy the journey.

V. Raghunathan
Academic, author, corporate citizen, columnist and hobbyist
Not necessarily in that order...
Bengaluru, India

Wit •ness to Mat•Haroo (मत• हारो) Spirit

Foreword: Lucio Muniain

Having the wonderful opportunity to write some words for Gurjit Singh Matharoo's book on his true-life events, which is co-authored by Vagish Naganur, the first thing that comes to my mind is to know that as of today we are two architects from opposite sides of the world, speaking in a way the same language. Architecture, in its innumerable shapes, stands as a testament to human creativity, resilience and the quest for meaning in an always evolving world. While all of us in the profession are embroiled in our own struggles to various degrees, to read a positive take on dealing with them is indeed refreshing.

Comparing Brutalism, Mexican Modernism and the works of Matharoo Associates offers a unique perspective on how architectural philosophies reflect broader existential and cultural narratives. Brutalism, with its raw concrete and imposing structures, emerges as a response to post-war pragmatism and a search for honesty in materials and form. Its stark, unadorned aesthetic is reminiscent of Soren Kierkegaard's existential musings: 'Life can only be understood backwards; but it must be lived forwards.' The Brutalist movement captures this tension between retrospection and forward momentum, a physical manifestation of existential struggle and resilience. In contrast, Mexican Modern Architecture brings a vibrant interplay of tradition and innovation, deeply rooted in cultural identity and social consciousness. As Alex Ross notes in his book *The Rest is Noise:* 'Art does not reflect culture; it produces it.' Mexican Modernism exemplifies this, producing an architectural language that is as much about cultural expression as it is about structural innovation. The colourful facades and organic forms are a dialogue between the past and the future, a celebration of national identity in a rapidly modernising world.

The contemporary work of Matharoo Associates bridges these historical and cultural divides with a pragmatic yet poetic approach to design. Through the stories, we get a peek into the process of how these ideas have developed, sometimes born through tiny instances that could have been easily missed or ignored. Their work, characterised by meticulous attention to detail and context, resonates with the ethos described by Henry Miller in his book *Black Spring:* 'One's destination is never a place, but a new way of seeing things.' Matharoo Associates' architecture offers new perspectives, transforming the ordinary into the extraordinary through innovative design solutions that respect and enhance their surroundings.

On the other hand, Beatriz Colomina argues in her book *Architecture Production and Reproduction:* 'Architecture is not simply a platform that accommodates the viewing subject. It is a viewing mechanism that produces the subject.' This idea is vividly illustrated in the works of all three architectural approaches discussed here. Brutalism, Mexican Modernism and the designs of Matharoo Associates all produce unique experiences for their inhabitants, shaping not just spaces, but the very perception of those who interact with them.

The stories remind us that ultimately, the successful architectural endeavours, no matter how grand or innovative, are deeply human at their core. They are products of our collective aspirations, struggles and creativity. They demonstrate that architecture, like all human efforts, is an ongoing dialogue between the individual and the collective, the past and the future. As we explore these distinct yet interconnected attempts, through the lucid storytelling by the authors, we see that the pursuit of architectural excellence is, indeed, only human after all.

Lucio Muniain
Painter, musician and architect. Collector of music and art.
Mexico City, Mexico

Wit •ness to Mat•Haroo (मत• हारो) Spirit

Author's Note: Vagish Naganur

I have known G (Gurjit Singh Matharoo) since the days I was a student, and he was my teacher, who gave one-liners or sometimes just one-word lessons at the School of Architecture[1]. One day, he was on the public phone at the School, maybe a distress call from a client, and as I was jaywalking past him, he pulled me over and asked me to join his studio. As destiny would have it, I ended up as a proud intern in his three-person studio.

Those were his struggling days, and with the practice gathering pace, a magazine approached him for an article on his work. He, instead, asked me to write something hurriedly. Just to avoid my discomfort with academic jargon, I said I would write about wit in his work, to which I was a key witness.

*

Wishing him on a special occasion with two consecutive wins, I said, 'Congrats, Gurjit! You got the *Young* Architect's Award *twice in a row!*'

'I think it's high time that they gave me the *Lifetime-Young* Architect's Award[2]!' Pat came the reply.

Soon he went on to win the most acclaimed International *Emerging* Architecture Award, that too, *twice in a row!*

---

1. Centre for Environmental Planning and Technology *and G's alma mater, is a premier institute of architecture and allied design in Ahmedabad.*
2. *This national award consists of the most coveted* Architect of the Year Award, *which G was denied. The other awards include the not so coveted* Young Architect of the Year Award *for those below 35 years of age, and the* Lifetime Achievement Award *for those above 60 years.*

*

While working on a riverside resort, a 100 foot mandatory margin[3] had to be left between the building and the river edge.

'The building cannot be close to the river, but no one said we can't bring the river close to the building!' said calm G. He then persuaded the clients to get a mining licence to blast off the rocks in between.

*

While designing a residence for a client, who turned out to be a Don, the prayer room was attached to the house by a long corridor, deliberately misaligned. I asked if the angle signified some cardinal reference.

'No! It is to say that the path they are on may not lead them to God,' he replied as a matter of fact.

*

These are some references from real-life anecdotes, which many of us encounter being with G. Wit as a way of dealing with life has been his trademark. Design process turns into a joyous exercise, with everybody chipping in 'wit-bits' and G trying to orchestrate it. Wit, according to me, is not avoiding or outsmarting the problem. Perhaps it is facing and answering it innovatively! Rather than a clichéd feeling that one gets from theoretical verbose, his approach instils a sense of playfulness with impeccable timing.

In the exhaustively serious profession of architecture, his practice comes across as light and refreshing. One can't even say 'jokes apart' as most jokes become part of the design itself. Many of his clients, be it diamantaires, dignitaries or divinitories, are surprised by his absurd logic but still start questioning their own. Many sloggers started taking midday naps, teetotallers became habitually spirited, while some ardent followers drifted

---

3. *Minimum distance from the site boundary that must be maintained without any building, as per local byelaws.*

away from spirituality.

The only way to follow him is to outwit him. You cannot replicate G, as all his thoughts are entwined in his multidimensional engagement with people, places and prejudices. He soon turns any problem-solving into a game of impossibilities, be it with family, friends or peers. The whole high is in playing the game without bending the rules. Many a time, these fuzzy logic puzzles become infectious for colleagues, contractors and even clients. When design demands and personality traits interlock, it evolves into an unforgettable anecdote.

The game was set. An idea had germinated. Over the last 30 years, internship grew into a friendship. I became a landscape consultant for most of his projects. My privilege has been meeting him, his people and his clients and knowing them up close and deep down. In the meantime, a common friend Rajesh Renganathan of Flying Elephant fame, with his limited command over Hindi, split apart Mat-haroo (Hindi for 'never lose') in G's last name and discovered a hidden spirit.

'My family and I will forever remain indebted to him, as we now cannot relax or call it a day anymore.' G grinned.

The seed has now sprouted into a collection of 30 odd anecdotes that bring forth more than 30 years of design battles fought with a witty sword, most lost and few drawn.

Vagish Naganur

Wit •ness to Mat •Haroo (मत• हारो) Spirit

Author's Note: Gurjit Singh Matharoo

I am grateful to friend and colleague Vagish for making me the scapegoat once again. He coined the word wit-ness and appended it to our practice, and now there is no escape from it. He has also conveniently appointed himself to the elevated position of *Sutradhar*, the ancient teller of stories - who can appear anytime, utter anything and disappear anywhere; turning, twisting and tweaking episodes at will. Anyway, all thanks to him, the stories we reminisce and relish in private are now out in the open.

True as far as memory hasn't failed us, put as softly as our clients can take it and made as gentle as possible for all our peers, masters and colleagues. He has taken liberty with the language to highlight the gravity of the situation, with blessings from all; Gods to gurus, monkeys to mankind, and of course women - in all their avatars; and that too with such dexterity that none will feel alarmed or offended, I trust. In any case we have been able to sufficiently un-*Google* the names and locations enough for them, so as to not trace themselves back to our stories.

Though not taught in any school of architecture, it is the clients that make or break us. The stories are about the strange and unusual ways that bond us architects with them. The unexpected calls from some of them after decades, exactly while we were in the process of compiling their stories, is testimony enough to the bizarre connections we establish. No story is complete without a salute to our earnest clients.

Vagish has allotted *Mirchis*[1] to the stories when the going gets tough. The novice reader, not accustomed to the dynamics of architectural practice, is advised to start with the least number

---

1. *Chillies, in Hindi; like in a menu card, the number used denotes the degree of difficulty for somebody not used to architectural vocabulary or practice.*

and move their way up the *Mirchis*. They may also follow the chronology or the links or read them in any manner they like. At the end of the day, he would have convinced you that sequence doesn't matter and blamed that on me too.

I thank Dilshad profusely, who joined us in the book journey and early morning conference laughing sessions that made us feel as if the Covid-19 lockdown was a vacation. The trio 'met' each morning in the dark when no one was awake, wrote from blue putridity to crumpled beds to wet love, but without ever seeing each other, thanks to our smart phones and free *Whatsapp*.

V.Raghunathan has been one of my favourite authors and his books have had me hooked for years. Presented in a lighter vein, they offer an acute insight into human behavioural patterns. I also feel connected to his mechanical bent of mind and lateral thinking for problem solving. To have a brilliant foreword from him - and for novice writers like us - is a great honour.

While Raghunathan's foreword is a dream come true, Lucio's makes us dream on. Sitting on my antipode, we are still able to share such a strong bond that the world seems like a much smaller place. His work is bold and poetic - truly inspiring. I'm overwhelmed with his placement of our work in the regions of thinkers and the link he establishes with the past and present of architecture. I can't thank him enough for his generosity.

Grateful to Anisha Chacko for designing the beautiful book cover and to Gordon Goff and his team at ORO Editions for taking this book to the outside world.

Thanks to my interns Manav, Trishla and Dhvani, who while editing my corrections, have all left a mark on the stories that even we may take years to unearth. An army was part of the process, including Sanjana, Kavan and Ankita. A special thank you to Sathwik - who slogged to put it all together and gave us our first test copies, printed and bound.

Not to forget my friends - especially Poonam, Urvi, Madhavi, Miki, Milind, Anshuman, Shilpa, Devangi and Ahaladini - who were all trapped into hearing us out and offer suggestions, both in and out of the pool. My thanks to the ever-sincere architect Trisha. Pulled into the trio, she meticulously rationalised each word, line, layer and meaning(s) to sort out our mess and bring sanity into this mayhem by putting a finite end to the book.

Finally, I remain indebted to architect and my wife, Komal, and adolescent children, Advay and Adyah, who had to bear the brunt of our rather loud readings at 6 a.m. every day, getting little snippets from the stories but never ever getting the whole picture.

No thank you is bigger than the thank you to my father Rajendra Singh Matharoo or PapaG as he is referred to in the book. He left us a few weeks before the book was published, leaving behind bittersweet memories. His thoughts and love, his pragmatic insights and his humour will stay with us forever.

Gurjit Singh Matharoo

Wit •ness to Mat •Haroo (मत• हारो) Spirit

You Don't Say NO to the Underworld

Prologue:

On April 26, 2020, during the Covid-19 nationwide lockdown, G picked five stories to send to friends for review. As an afterthought, he decided this story should be added too. At 8 p.m., just as he was forwarding it, his phone rang. He was shocked to see the caller's name. It was someone he had known a few decades ago, when it had all begun. We will come back to this dreaded phone call, but for now, let's time travel to those days.

Once upon a time in the Megapolis-on-an-Island...

Contact X confirmed that a rendezvous had been fixed; that too, with none other than the Don himself. G was hesitant but still excited about working with exotic locales, unlimited budgets and absolute free will - or so he assumed!

The Don owned a valley - not a barren one, but a lush green one - not by the river side, but with a river that flowed through the middle of the site. With nothing on record, G started with a clean slate and worked head over heels, following just his instincts. It was, however, known only to a few of us close to him, that his design for the Don's house was a queer mix of works by his past Masters, Corb[1]-Ando[2]-Scarpa[3], stirred into one potent mocktail.

---

1. *Le Corbusier. French-Swiss architect, one of the pioneers of modern architecture.*
2. *Tadao Ando. Japanese architect, best known for minimalistic concrete buildings.*
3. *Carlo Scarpa. Italian architect, whose exquisite architecture was based on collaborations with craftsmen.*

Finally, as D-Day arrived, he was summoned to the Megapolis-on-an-Island. Contact X cautioned that they would be face-to-face with the Don and his younger brother - the next of kin, if the former didn't exist, a likely possibility in those days of frequent encounters with the police. G and Contact X arrived at the Don's fortified den carrying a large suspicious looking parcel.

G had been sufficiently warned by Contact X before the meeting. 'You are aware of what they do. Good, but never bring it up...'
'If your opinion differs from theirs, no problem! Just keep it to yourself...'
'They will offer payments in *hawala*[4], *matter*[5] or even *supari*[6]. Accept only in *hari patti*[7], never in kind.'

G's mind was full of *khokas*[8] and *petis*[9], as they were ushered into the air-conditioned den. A chill went down his spine.

The Don seemed more dreadful than India's three most iconic villains, Mogambo-Gabbar-Shakaal, put together. G forgot all about the concrete building he was proposing and instead had the excruciating desire to cast the Don as the last and ultimate Hindi movie villain.

The Don and the brother turned out to be unusually pleasant and sweet, going gaga over the building model taken out of the parcel and soon the deal was sealed.

'Let's go out and have lunch,' said the Don in celebration.

It was too good and had happened too soon. G privately pinched himself to make sure it was not a dream and then secretly bowed down in reverence to his past Masters, Corb-Ando-Scarpa. The mood was light and cheerful. But can one escape destiny?

4. *Illegal value transfer in Hindi and Underworld lingo.*
5. *A situation in English. Dispute redressal in Underworld lingo.*
6. *Betel nut in Hindi. Contract killing in Underworld lingo.*
7. *Green leaves in Hindi. Hard cash in Underworld lingo.*
8. *Crate in Hindi. Crore or 10 million in illegal cash in Underworld lingo.*
9. *Suitcase in Hindi. Lac or 100 thousand in illegal cash in Underworld lingo.*

On the way out, the duo bumped into their friend, who had come calling.

'Meet Our Doctor Z,' introduced the Don, and after basic pleasantries, he turned around and said, 'Doctor, come see the beautiful house Our Architect is making for us.'

G had now become 'Our Architect.'

They all walked back into the den. Doctor Z glanced at the model and after a deep sigh that lasted a millisecond, proclaimed aloud, 'Don't you think it looks like a *tabela*[10]?'

The mood in the room turned sombre.

Instantly, all smiles were wiped off! G felt a shooting pain in his chest, triggered by a doctor himself.

'It does look like a *tabela*,' said the Don, who changed sides 180 degrees, just like a Hindi movie climax, and was now facing G.

'Oh! So true, I didn't think of it,' seconded the younger. He too turned around, leaving G alone without cover or accomplice. Contact X was silently fading into the background.

Those felt like piercing shots to G, who was by now already down and under. In no time, his dreams were splattered all over.

In the severe pain, he felt it was a grave insult to his past Masters, Corb-Ando-Scarpa.

The brother went inside and brought out an old blueprint[11], with a cheap imitation of a colonial villa. The hexagonal plan with symmetrical sloping roofs and an ornate façade was a far cry from the modern aesthetic G had grown up with.

---

10. *Cow shed in Hindi.*
11. *A reproduction print of a building drawing. All architects' drawings were issued in this form using ammonia, before the advent of electronic printers.*

The encounter wasn't over yet!

Poking the muzzle on G's gunshot wounds, the brother decreed, 'We all like this design, just add a few more rooms!'

Within moments, they had turned the aspiring architect into a Xerox[12] machine. G was outraged; it was blasphemy. The design inspired by his Masters was now mere cow dung. His last desire was to throw those prints back at them and turn their faces blue.

Sensing G's extinction, Contact X pulled him into the background. 'Remember! You swore not to voice your opinion.'

Swallowing his pride, G kept *maun*[13] and they left the den dejected. His only consolation was that he was a qualified, independent, registered architect who could choose who to work for, at his own free will. 'To hell with them! I never wanted to work for these goons! Good, your plan didn't work.' G turned 180 degrees too.

'You don't say No to the Underworld!' said Contact X with calm, 'Didn't I tell you?'

He had not, and now it was too late.

A few months later, I saw the project on the drawing board at the M-Ass-Studio⁺, in the Beloved-city-of-A-Bad.

'Oh! Still at it?' I instigated him a bit. 'Let's see your hexa-goons.'

The drawing had a central passage with rooms on either side. It continued out of the house and abruptly turned a few degrees, only to terminate in a shrine. Intrigued with the slight change in the direction of the passage, I asked, 'Why this sudden turn? Aligned to some cardinal direction or sacred place?'

+ *Refer to the story, 'Only Time Would Tell,' page 111*
12. *Pioneers of photocopiers in India. Xerox is the brand name used as a generic term.*
13. *A vow of silence in Sanskrit.*

4

'No! It is to say that the path they are on may not lead them to God.' He replied as a matter of fact.

'Hmm…' I had to warn him, 'With this twisted approach of yours, they'll make sure You soon reach God!'

*

G's early learnings came from the Underworld, although this association was short-lived. As fate would have it, the Don and his brother were shot dead in an inter-gang shootout. Contact X faded further into the background. Doctor Z was arrested under TADA[14] for taking a bullet out of an escaping fugitive who was shot by the police.

'You don't say No to the Underworld,' had applied to Doctor Z too.

Epilogue:

Let's go back to the dreaded 8 p.m. call during the nationwide lockdown:

'Kaisa hai?'[15]

'Sab khariyat hai bhai! Achanak kaise phone…?'[16] *G didn't want to mention that he had just pulled out the Don story.*

'Bas. Teri yaad aayee!'[17]

With Doctor Z in jail and the Don and his brother dead in 1998, G hardly had any contact with Contact X or the Underworld. Who could the caller be?

It was the youngest and third of the Don Brothers! Let's call him Y!

---

14. *Terrorist and Disruptive Activities (Prevention) Act. A severe Indian anti-terrorism law in force from 1985-1995.*
15. *'How are you?' in Hindi.*
16. *'All good brother! How come you called all of a sudden?' in Hindi.*
17. *'Just. Was remembering you!' in Hindi.*

The Secret Society of Broke Masons

It was the night of Equinox; the Moon was faint and foxes howled far off in the horizon. Golden yellow light glowed through a clearing in the thicket of *babool*[1] and *neem*[1]. The wind was warm and thick, and an air of suspicion lingered around...

First, the men with tools started trickling in. As they got busy, the middle order arrived to monitor the scene with a hawk's eye. There would be no second chance.

Magic potion was being brewed for the midnight cult ritual. With the right mix, correct proportions, perfect moisture and precise temperature, the viscous concoction was ready. G walked in and made customary titbits by poking, rubbing and nosing it. The team leader came last and checked the status, while everyone greeted and acknowledged him with a certain uncertainty. The sceptical Client MM was mum, of course, while architects from M-Ass-Studio stood perplexed.

The place was spick and span, and now completely sealed off. The *karigar*[2] was freshly bathed and ready. The night of reckoning for The Secret Society of Broke Masons had beckoned. As the owl hooted in the vicinity, G made a hand gesture. The ritual was on. Thus began a perfect night: the Moon now shining round and bright.

The ritual of casting concrete is sacred to the M-Ass-Studio. As things

---

1. *Wild medicinal trees commonly found in rural parts of India.*
2. *Sought after artisan in Hindi.*

remain just as they are cast, it better be done to its best. It's almost like recording songs without acoustic insulation in those HMV[3] days. I heard they would do it at a stretch in the dead of night to avoid unwanted noise. If all went well, great! Or one had to start all over again. However, this luxury of retake is not available while casting in concrete, even though it is said that architecture is frozen music[4].

As the space was conceived to be monolithic, the flooring had to be in cement concrete too. G had spent his childhood in a house that had shiny cement floors, but there are few takers for this dying art today. He had called upon a Friend from the Megapolis-on-an-Island who was designing expensive houses, albeit with traditional methods; here was G, designing frugal houses with whatever methods. The Friend's team would turn out to be too expensive for G's floor and the best way to cut costs was that G followed his instructions to the T, while working with his own people.

G had called the Friend a few days before execution.

'Note them down. You'll forget.' The Friend had his elaborate instructions by heart.

'Of course, I won't forget. I am getting a Rs.200 per square foot floor for just Rs.20,' G assured.

'It's sensitive. Don't be casual!' said the Friend, for whom floor casting was his monopoly and trade secret.

'I won't!' G promised.

'Okay! First, the temperature has to be right, 25 to 30 degrees! Including yours!'

---

3. *His Master's Voice was a major British record label created in 1901 by* The Gramophone Co. Ltd. *The phrase is from the title of a painting depicting a terrier-mix dog named Nipper listening to a wind-up disc gramophone.*
4. *'Music is liquid architecture; architecture is frozen music.' Johann Wolfgang von Goethe, 18th century German writer.*

'...Where will I get matching temperatures and that too so low?' G smiled.

'Start at midnight. No heat, no dust, no scratch. You can't leave marks on my flooring.' By now, it was already the possessive Friend's flooring.

'MIDNIGHT?'

'The *karigar* should have slept well and shouldn't be overfed. If he is drowsy, You are finished, not the floor.'

'*Karigars* don't sleep during the day. Should I try singing him a lullaby?'

'No jokes! You can't change the *karigar* midway!'

'Done with your diktats?' G was now restless.

'NO! Be patient! Start from one end, even strokes throughout, come out of the other!'

'How do I know he is doing it right?' G tried hard to be humble.

'One look and you'll know. Just laid: it'll be smooth as silk, glistening like sweat!'

'A sweaty one?' G was floored.

'Yes! And don't use normal water, it'll leave salt behind. Only bottled!'

'What? *Bisleri*[5]? Okay. Will tell all to bring their own.' G thought the Friend was going overboard with the water, but realised that you don't charge 10 times for mere cement flooring just like that; you do need to go overboard.

---

5. *Pioneer of bottled water in India. Bisleri is the brand name used as a generic term.*

This was days before. G had crammed his tutorials well. Let's go back to that glorious midnight, to the gathering of The Secret Society of Broke Masons.

The casting ritual was seamless - correct sequence, perfect concoction, precise viscosity, bathed *karigar*, even strokes from one end to the other - all synchronised to the chorus of the cult, no words.

As the *karigar* walked out after his last stroke, the world stood still. The floor glistened like a perfect mirror. One could see all the members of The Secret Society of Broke Masons in pensive calm, reflected upside-down in it. Everyone wished each other goodbye and prepared to call it a night. Now, they only had to wait some hours for the flooring to harden.

The Moon had reached its zenith. Just then, out of the blue, right in the middle of the soft, wet, shiny floor, almost like an apparition, appeared a...Dog!!?

Everyone froze. Nobody had seen anything like it before, and within moments, The Secret Society of Broke Masons was in shambles.

'Sshhhh! No one makes a sound, if it sits or runs - game over,' whispered one.

The situation had turned into a Catch 22[6]. Get it excited, it may run; make it comfortable, it'll settle right there. Sweet talk was the only soft walk out.

'They like the sound of squeaky toys,' said a dog expert broke mason. 'Sequeak! Squeeek!' rhymed the other, imitating a toy.

'Wait! It looks lost. Let me try. Muahch! Muach! Much! Umah!' Another started to kindle affection by making kissing sounds.

---

6. *A paradoxical situation from which one cannot escape. It was coined in 1961 by American author Joseph Heller in his satirical war novel* Catch 22.

'Careful! It's liking it. It might sit there and cast itself.'
'Let me try. Does anyone have a bone?'
'Is there a puppy around to calm it down?'
The situation had turned the secret society into dog whisperers instantly.

'All our endeavours have been for nought. What did we do in life to deserve this?' The broke masons started losing hope.

'The longer it stands, the deeper will be the footprints.' Newtonian laws were being formulated.

Their collective calibre, careful considerations and computed calculations had not prepared them for this contingent calamity. Life had never been so precarious before and would never be the same again. In an instant, The Secret Society of Broke Masons had now become a Clueless Conglomeration of Canine Cuddlers.

The Dog, however, would not trust men who had turned lovers over a one-night stand. Not used to such affection being showered, it instead chose solitary freedom. While the discussions on levitating strategies and honey trappings got intense, the Dog, exactly like it had appeared…vanished from the scene!

For a moment, everyone was as frozen as the Dog had been. Such was their plight that they could not even access the spot to assess the damage, not knowing what sin had been committed or what tomorrow held for them. They started dispersing slowly with a deafening silence in their minds; the Moon had turned its palest.

That night, there was introspection. What led to this apocalypse? Who caused the catastrophe? Was it treason by one of the broke masons? Just plain manhandling? Or was the viscous potion vicious? One of them remembered tripping over a cursed lemon in the morning, while another believed it was G's cheating with the *Bisleri*. One suspected adultery in the cult, some others felt it was black magic of the occult. The conglomerate, however, remained clueless.

The obsessive, possessive Friend called the next morning. 'How was it?'

'Okay...'

'Was the mix right?'

'Yesss...'

'*Karigar* fresh?'

'Of course...'

'When all good, why just okay?'

'...a dog walked on it...'

'WHAT??? A DOG?!! WHAT!! DAMN! You were not to allow a speck of dust and you walked a DOG on it?'

'Not me. Just the dog!'

'Don't call me for anything ever again!' the Friend slammed the phone down. He however, raised the cost of his flooring by another 10% and added another commandment to his long SOP[7] list - No dogs on freshly laid flooring.

*

What happened to the Friend?
That was the end of the Friend's friendship; his floor had hit the roof.

The house?
It won the 'Best House in the World' Award, an architectural wonder visited by many.

---

7. *Standard Operating Procedure.*

And The Secret Society of Broke Masons?
Not a secret anymore, they continued to be broke.

Some essential questions will always remain unanswered.
Why was the dog there? Who sent him? Sent him for what?

Was the dog Dharma[8]?

Even to this day,
Only a few see,
Stamped on the floor,
Footprints divine...

---

8. *The dog that accompanied the Pandavas during their last days was actually the*
    Supreme Lord in the form of Yama - the God of Death, who tested Yudhisthira as
    he was ascending to Heaven. From Book 17 Chapter 3 - Mahaprasthanika Parva,
    Mahabharata.

Wit •ness to Mat •Haroo (मत• हारो) Spirit

The Old Monk Who Bought Gin-O-Logi
🌶

'Try this! It's morning catch. My fisherman got it specially for you!'

This is from the time when the Don Brothers were not yet dead[+]. G was getting spoilt; fortnightly seaside site visits were becoming an addiction with the Don's offerings and their warm hospitality.

The only thing G longed for was some spice in practice, some wild design opportunity. And one day, there it was! On the table, in the M-Ass-Studio, lay an invite to a design competition[1] for a 5 lac[2] square foot University of J Religious Studies, which would be the largest of its kind in the world. Institutes are architects' wet dreams - those excessive interactive spaces, that philosophical base. And the Js? He knew a bit about them. They are the richest business community. Maybe the Underworld had possessed more than them, but Js would pay with kindness, not in kind, thought the overzealous G.

Now the catch! The initiator of this unique University was an Acharya *- not like the caricature, larger than life gurus we see all over social media, but a real-life learned scholar. The design would only be of his choice and his brief was simple: a campus based purely on the tenets of the J religion.*

The submission deadline was a mere 45 days, within which G

+   *Refer to the story, 'You Don't Say NO to the Underworld,' page 1*
1. *Architecture Design Competition, which gives architects the chance to be recognised and win public project commissions.*
2. *Equivalent to 100 thousand.*

would have to study and understand the religion, before applying it to something he had never attempted before - an enormous campus design. A large number of drawings were needing to be produced, and not to forget, an impressive double bed size model which would be the show stealer. He would be competing against the best in the business and could afford no loose ends. G knew a bit about J's but nothing of their religion. Poles apart, he was from the modest warrior S religion background.

'How can you go against your own religion of Modernism?' I provoked him.

'We won't. We will do the best campus design we can, this is the day we were waiting for!' G was deliberately trying to ignore the point.

'Maybe you missed it: their only brief is a design based on J tenets. They are not even looking for a modern architect.' I opined, knowing well that he had already given up on winning; he only wanted beautiful drawings for his archives.

'Leave the J religion to me!' was his war cry.

Not understanding his high-handedness, we went back to our drawing boards and immersed ourselves in creating a great campus. Half the duration was over, it was now time to start the final presentation drawings. J tenets were nowhere in sight.

'We haven't yet met any expert, nor studied J temple architecture and haven't even tried to know about the religion.' Time was ticking, I had to remind him.

'I have to go for the Don's site visit,' and off he escaped to the world under. On his return, fully charged from his weekend site visit, he went straight to the School[3] library and picked up a large book on J mythological paintings.

---

3. G's alma mater.

'Ohh! A picture book? You don't stand a chance against the other architects.'

'Wait! Can we pick out paintings roughly matching our plans?'

So illogical! But we went along. The book was a holy grail of paintings with captions - it was easy and didn't even take half an hour! We found at least one painting similar to each building we had designed and one similar to the campus layout too!

'Great! Let's shoot them.'

Although we needed only 12 matching images, to avoid any wastage of film, he shot the entire roll of 36 frames[4] from his macro lens[5] camera acquired during his days in the Land-of-Watches-and-Banks. The book was promptly returned to the library. G's reasoning: 'Deserving students may need it more than us!'

In two days, we received all 36 contact prints[6] of 1.5 X 1.5 inches size from the photo processing lab; most that were redundant and a few that matched the buildings.

'Now all we need to do is insert one diagram between each building plan and the chosen corresponding painting!'

'Oh! You will play the slides backward and show the painting transforming into a building! Reversing the fundamental inspiration-to-creation sequence?'

'Yes! Let's effect the Cause!'

---

4. *Maximum number of photographs possible on a single roll of film in an analogue camera, before the advent of digital technology.*
5. *A camera lens that specifically allows close up photography of small subjects. When photographing architectural models, it is able to capture what being in the space would feel like.*
6. *Small sized photographic images produced from the roll of film by direct placement on a single sheet of photo paper and without enlargement. It was used as a reference guide to develop the photographs into a larger size.*

It was unsettling for me initially, until I remembered his mantra[7]. *For G, the logical sequence didn't matter as long as pieces fell into the right place. However, all his codes,* mantras *and thinking caps could never sort one thing out - the submission deadline! It was always* Mission: Impossible *for us!*

'Wish you had told us before, there is no time left for the model.'

'We won't make the usual double bed size, just an A3[8]!'

'Nuts! No study of J and now, a full campus on a bedside table. Monks will reject us just on the quantum of material.'

The minuscule paper model was ready in four days. Four storeys were just four inches high. In the meantime, G asked for his briefcase to be pulled out from the loft.

'Oh! Carrying the model in a briefcase? Saving on freight too?' I knew the small model wouldn't be even a tad bit impressive.

'Don't worry, the briefcase isn't for the model.' G had other ideas.

'Better not be, your modern barren walls will never get selected.' I tried being pragmatic, hoping against hope.

G paused for a second and inquired, 'Where are those redundant contact prints of the paintings?'

'Besides the ones already used to show as inspiration-After-design? Now what?'

'Let's stick them on the walls in the model. Why waste them?'

The remaining contact prints were neatly cut out and stuck on some of the blank façades in the model. Silent like monks, we worked like machines. A sponge sheet was dipped in cups of

---

7. *Motivating chant in Sanskrit.*
8. *Standard paper size of 11.7 x 16.5 inches.*

leftover tea and used as desert landscape. Finally, it was picture-perfect. Now, his macro lens was being used to take close-up shots of the model.

'We are not carrying the model.' G spoke through the lens.

'*Santhara*[9] already? What are you up to?' I tried to reason.

'Not carrying drawings too!' said G in renouncement.

'You going *digambara*[10]? Oh. It's not even *santhara*, it's *hara-kiri*[11]... and that too, with Our sweat and blood!'

Anyway, the show must go on and so it did. At the venue, the *svetambara*[12] monks were shaken too. In their campus full of white marble and bright light, G had requested for a completely dark room and was walking in with a briefcase carrying just the projector and his only emergency backup - an additional projector bulb.

It was a gathering of 50 monks headed by the revered *Acharya* himself, the J equivalent of the Dalai Lama. All white, trapped in a dark room. The only ray of hope left was the light from the projector beaming across. G had memorised the painting captions and simply narrated them with the corresponding slides. There was a stunned silence. No sound...other than the cooling fan of the slide projector.

The presentation was dazzling. In the dark, the building plans seemed to appear out of the chosen paintings. Texture on the paper model looked like traditional stone construction, and the unevenly tea-soaked sponge looked like actual sand dunes in the distance. The waste contact prints?

---

9. *It is the Jain religious practice of voluntarily fasting to death by gradually reducing the intake of food and liquids.*
10. *Sky-clad in Sanskrit. One of the two main sects of Jainism and refers to the traditional practice of neither possessing nor wearing any clothes.*
11. *Japanese ritual suicide by self-disembowelment on a sword.*
12. *One of the two main sects of Jainism and refers to the traditional practice of wearing white clothes.*

They appeared like giant J murals on lofty stone walls!

The project was indeed awarded to us.

Later, in private, the *Acharya* asked G just one question, 'Most of the younger monks present could not comprehend the J theories you brought forth. It takes a lifetime for such a deep understanding of our religious concepts. I'm at a loss as to how you arrived at such sublime knowledge, that too, in just 45 days.'

'Not 45 Guruji, just 1.' G wanted to correct him, but didn't. In the nick of time, he was reminded of the value of *maun* from his underworld Don clients[+].

With projector in hand and project in lap, G had to open a current account with a bank, overnight. It had to have a name too.

'Something-Associates it will be, so it seems like a large firm.' We went about designing a letterhead in sepia and black – as the *Xerox*[13] machine those days could copy only these two colours, that too, one after the other on the same sheet.

M-Ass was born.

G already had a long association with the word. His Montessori school, run by two Anglo-Indian ladies, had a name that abbreviated to ASS. These letters were boldly and permanently embroidered on the long ties of the uniform, which the children wore with pride. So, since his childhood, G has been very comfortable wearing the label around his neck.

The next weekend, G left for his site visit and narrated the entire incident, of design first and inspiration later, to the Don.

'Ohhh, so you shot first, then drew the bull's-eye around it! You are the arrived One!'

+   *Refer to the story, 'You Don't Say NO to the Underworld,' page 1*
13. *Pioneers of photocopiers in India. Xerox is the brand name used as a generic term.*

Only then it Don-ed upon G...

The randomly picked paintings had broken the usual sequential order of learning, making the *Acharya* believe that G had actually studied and internalised the entire course; it impressed the *Acharya* so much that during later site visits, he would call the waiting G out from the audience to sit on the dais beside him. With the disciples performing *sashtang pranam*[14] just a few feet away from him, cross-legged G would feel very uncomfortable.

With glasses in hand, I questioned this strange approach that had made things fall into place when G returned to the Beloved-city-of-A-Bad.

'Should we call it G-no-Logic[15] or just neat Gin-o-Logi?'

'First, you turn yourself into a work-o-holic!'

'Why? Are you finally joining the old monk?' I nudged.

'Join him? I can't even sit cross-legged!'

But G kept crossing legs between Dons and Monks for a period of two years. Both projects fell apart with the passing of the Acharya *and the Don Brothers getting killed.*

Clients alive no more, projects gone with the wind, no balance in the current account.

M-Ass was truly born!

---

14. *Paying respect by lying fully prostrate on the floor with arms stretched out in front towards God, or a person in authority.*
15. *When read, interpreted in Gujarati as G's-logic, or in English as G-without-logic.*

Wit •ness to Mat •Haroo (मत• हारो) Spirit

Believing is Seeing
🌶

Coco wore a lacy top and her hair was in two pigtails, tied up with pink and blue clips. She was always dressed in colourful clothes and always delighted to be on site. Maybe it was the sea breeze and the limitless environs in contrast to her South-Megapolis-on-an-Island apartment. She walked around inquisitively while the client, A, went about her business of taking stock of things. Even though Coco was cheerful and A fiery in her approach, everybody was still wary of Coco and in silent adoration of A; blame it on Coco's unpredictability and A's charm in an otherwise harsh and rugged construction environment.

Today's site visit had gone alright, with no major scene being created: Coco not throwing tantrums and A surprisingly not having too many points of discontent. The sun was setting on the Sea-of-Arabia and the visit coming to a close. G, with his gang of D, R and me, all felt that today was the perfect day to finally bring up the seaside fencing. Even before we could muster the courage to say it, the mercurial lady A uttered the impossible, 'I need a high boundary wall and want the view of the sea!'

Even such drastic contradictory needs and wants seemed perfectly reasonable from the gracious A on that sultry evening. The boundary wall on the seaside had to address a strange mix of concerns: security, transparency and a pest-proof barrier. G, instead of taking it up as a new challenge to solve the impossible, had thought of keeping it simple and practical.

'We have decided to do a simple chain-link fence. The sea is not obstructed and we will have basic security too.' G blurted without pause. It was perhaps a mix of delayed payments and a penchant for his afternoon nap that was missed, playing on his mind.

'Of course! I want the sea, but what on earth is chain-link???'

Fortunately, it was not a clear 'no' from her, as was normally the case. Today was an unusual day; instead of it becoming a design problem, the discussion had now drifted to another level of complexity: explaining a mundane chain-link to an elite client, whose attention to technicalities could be measured in milliseconds.

'It's a kind of steel net tied between vertical poles,' G tried to explain - but in vain - certain that this decision would be left for another stressful day.

'No! You will have to show it to me.' A was adamant, while Coco, standing along with us, looked curiously from a distance.

With no *Google*, just the sea and the mangroves, how would G produce chain-link right there on the beach? That, and, within a few minutes? It seemed like a lost opportunity. Seeing his helplessness, Coco and the project team could only wait in exasperation. G looked around, knowing fully well that it was turning into a futile discussion. And just then, there was divine intervention. Lady Luck was on his side. Just 50 feet away, the adjoining property was marked with a chain-link fence, with only its vertical supports visible from where they stood. G pointed towards it with lightning alacrity!

'You see those poles? Completely see-through! That's what we call a chain-link fence!'

'Yeah, that will do!' agreed A. After which, she packed and left the site, with Coco in joyous agreement.

There was a sense of jubilation, and G wanted to share it with all the team members, who were now gathering around him as the clients had left. But since the neera[1] *kiosks would be closed this late, the celebration was going to be limited to just an extra* vada pav[2].

'What was it that you were showing her?' I asked, having heard their discussion from a distance.

'That chain-link there. She approved it, didn't you see?' G wanted to close the matter with no further debate.

'WHAT CHAIN? WHAT LINK??? ONLY POLES!'

'What???' Astonished G started walking towards the bushy, deserted neighbouring property, with us in tow. Indeed, the fence was all long gone. Only the rusted poles remained. He then instructed me to grow thorny bushes in the area, so no one else would be able to come close and realize.

Anyway, this delusion allowed my landscape design to continue unabated to the beach and on to the sea. With A and her fire gone, it would be this calm union of the Panchamahabhoot[3] *with sky, earth, water and air that I would be dealing with. I thanked the all-pervading, invisible, non-existent, humble chain-link fence! It was indeed divine, for Believing Is Seeing!*

Having already seen that there was no fence in the adjoining property, Coco turned out to be the most farsighted of us all. Thinking of the endless territory that would be bestowed upon her, it was with joyous approval that she had wagged her tail.

---

1. *Palm nectar in Hindi. The sap extracted from the tree is a local alcoholic drink.*
2. *A vegetarian fast-food dish native to the state of Maharashtra. It consists of a fried potato and coriander dumpling, placed inside a half-sliced bun.*
3. *The group of five elements that is the basis of all cosmic creation.*

Karmic Alliance
🌶 🌶

One fine morning, a fresh graduate walked into M-Ass-Studio, with the intent to work with G.

'Unfortunately, there are no vacancies at present.'

Dejected, the girl left.

We'll come back to this dejection later, when the time is ripe. Let's now travel back many years to a time when G was trying to get a foothold in the Beloved-city-of-A-Bad.

He was on the verge of realising his first house in this city of dream houses. Against the norm of a squarish house with a garden in the front, he had been able to convince the Clients of his idea of a thin linear house with a 20 foot garden all along its side. However, more and more functional demands were added during the course of the design, the house swelled and swallowed the garden, which became slimmer by the day. So much so, that it was reduced to a miserly 12 feet wide. This wasn't good enough, so G put on his lateral thinking cap.

'Can't you buy another 10 foot strip from your neighbour's empty plot?' he suggested to his Clients.

'What? From the neighbours? We don't know who they are, have never even seen them! Heard they live in the U.S. of A.'

'No harm trying!' Drooling G left them tempted.

A few months later, the Clients did manage to buy the additional 10 foot strip from their invisible neighbours, the famed NRGs[1]. It surely was a case of matching the plot to suit G's design, and not the house to plot, as we are taught and practice. The project went into the construction phase. So far, so good.

Architect M frantically called G when she reached the house site to oversee the first slab[2] casting. The Client's brother-in-law was also the engineer on site, who, on his own whim and contrary to the drawings, was ready to cast an additional portion of the slab. This would completely ruin the main idea of a double height family space that was overlooking the long garden.

'At any cost, don't let them cast! Let me talk to the Client,' was G's command. The Client, who being a bureaucrat, was by now unreachable. He turned to me, 'She's alone, you also go to site. Hold that slab casting!' Desperate G needed manpower.

I rushed to the site to help M, to try and stop this over-faithful brother-in-law, who was adamant on spoiling the house. It was real-time action for newbies like M and me. Sometime later, we hesitantly called G from a STD.ISD.PCO[3], 'We tried our best. He didn't budge. The casting has begun.'

G was really disturbed. His first house was ruined. He would have to wait longer for his dream house in this city of dream houses. He later met and told the Client, 'We can't work with you anymore.'

For G, everything was lost - his first project in the Beloved-city-of-A-Bad, his name and money of course. In architecture, you can have your money or your ideals, not both.

---

1. *Non-Resident Gujarati. Often refers to the affluent Gujarati community who are Indian citizens but living outside the country.*
2. *The horizontal structural plane that forms the floor and ceiling.*
3. *Subscriber Trunk Dialling. International Subscriber Dialling. Public Call Office. From the mid to the late 90s, the yellow public telephone booths with STD.ISD. PCO written in black were the primary source of telecommunication before the advent of pagers and mobile phones.*

Those were the early days of G's practice, M-Ass-Studio was small and intimate. The few projects we had were hand-drafted on large drawing boards, giving them a touch, personal and human. M and I would cycle to the office while G arrived royal on his Bullet[4]. *Our plans were grand and we rode high!*

Sadly, the client who put in so much effort to acquire the extra land to nurture a G design, had killed it himself. The only saving grace was that this architectural activism brought M and me together, and G was proud of successfully creating the first all M-Ass-Studio alliance.

7 years had passed in this design city of 70,00,000 people, and G landed his second Client for a house. After initial discussions, G asked, 'How large is your plot?'

'We have two plots of 50 x 100 feet, so approximately 100 x 100 feet. A perfect square!' he exclaimed happily.

'That's nice! We will have enough garden all around.' G was keen on green.

Happy that there was another time and chance, he looked forward to their first site visit. As the site grew nearer, G had this queasy feeling. They were closing in on the botched-up house of the previous client that G had abandoned. G's eyes slowly closed shut.

'Oh wait!' The Client seemed to remember something. Awakened G held his breath.

'Years ago, our neighbours had called us. Their architect wanted a small strip of our plot to make their garden wider. We used to live in the U.S. of A with no intention of coming back, so I had agreed and sold it off to him. Our plot is actually 90 x 100 feet now. Not a perfect square.' Now he was 10% less happy, while G

---

4. Royal Enfield Bullet 350. *Known for its macho association, this street bike from 1932 is the longest running motorcycle in continuous production worldwide.*

was completely dumbstruck and cursing his fate.

Your past karma[5] *haunts you in strange ways. Now this Client found his chopped plot a bit too narrow for his liking. G's alliance with the land and payback was still pending. G let go of his breath slowly and started looking for his lateral thinking cap again.*

'The adjoining plot is vacant. Why don't you buy that?'

'What?? Penance for what we did years ago?' said the Client smilingly, unaware of G's own cruel entrapment with destiny.

'No harm trying!' G hadn't learnt his lesson and was still plotting on chopping adjacent plots.

The Client genuinely tried his best and came back a few days later. 'The adjoining plot is not available. Let's look for another property outside of the city.'

Years flew by. During this time, M and I were blessed with a beautiful daughter. Another all M-Ass-Studio alliance also took place. This time, it was for G himself[+].

NRGs no longer, the Clients did come back after a large plot of land was acquired. By now, the client's son had grown up to become the new client. Finally, G's dream house started. It was going smoothly, coming up nicely and the entire family was happy. Just before the finishing works were to commence, there was a sudden break.

'We will stop the construction for three months, I am getting married,' announced the young New Client.

'What has a wedding got to do with brick and mortar?' G said to himself. G is extremely skittish about construction breaks; the early episodes probably still hound him.

+ *Refer to the story, 'Wet Love,' page 105*
5. *In Hinduism, it is the relationship between a person's mental or physical action and the consequences that follow it.*

'Congratulations! Let's continue after the wedding!' was, however, all that G could mutter.

G was invited to the wedding reception, and he went to greet the newlywed couple. Destiny, too, had its own plot. The bride was none other than the same dejected graduate!

The time was indeed ripe. In this karmic alliance, she appeared in a fresh avatar, as his Newest Client!

Wit •ness to Mat •Haroo (मत• हारो) Spirit

Registrar of Death

The phone rang.

The sun disappeared and it was suddenly overcast at the M-Ass-Studio. Architect C picked up the phone, 'Hello! May I know who I'm speaking to?'

'Registrar of Death, Sir! Can you please get me G?'

A black crow pecked on the mirror. Bedevilled Architect C swiftly passed on the phone to G while covering the mouthpiece. 'Says he is somebody to do with death.'

Down below, the river too turned turbid. G took the phone from Architect C.

'Hell-oh!'

'This is the Registrar of Death, Sir. Can you hear me?'

'Loud and clear. Hope all is well?'

'Managing 50 bodies on a good day, Sir. Nothing short of 20- even on a lean one!'

'Way to go. Deadly numbers!'

'By the grace of the Almighty! Everybody's days are numbered, Sir. Drop in sometime.'

'Soon. You called for that?'

'Just wanted to confirm if I have your correct number.'

'Yes! Even my operator is the same.'

'Sir, there is a request to call you. Shall I pass?'

'Sure. Pass on.'

G was no stranger to death. Some years back, he had had no choice but to have snacks during daylong meetings, while bodies burnt all around. Those were the days of site visits to his gas-fired Crematorium that was replacing an old wood-fired one in the City-of-Diamonds. Of course, cremations could not be stopped while the new building was being constructed. Anyway, we will come back to this life-altering phone call later.

For now, let's travel to one of the funerals at his award-winning Crematorium, earlier that day.

PS was there, attending the last rites of a worker from his factory. It was a mere coincidence that he had recently met two prolific architects for the design of his large upcoming house. While one claimed 40 years of experience in designing houses, PS thought his buildings lacked Soul. The second one is known for his good taste in life. Just after their first meeting, PS was offered wine to toast. This had not gone down well with his teetotaller ways, and he felt that the architect did not have the right Spirit.

Anyway, fate ended up bringing him to the Crematorium with time to kill, till the worker's body turned to ash. They say that when someone goes to a death ceremony, one usually looks back at their own life, but here was PS, pondering upon the two architects' missing Soul and Spirit. While in the Crematorium, high on architecture, his soul seemed to have found the right spirit.

Sitting in this calm space by the river, he may have reflected within, 'If an architect can create a great lounge for departing souls, he sure can provide a comfortable one for the living!'

I don't know what exactly transpired within him or what he saw in a bare Crematorium that made him instantly rush to the chamber of the Registrar of Death. Let's leave PS in the chamber for now and jump a few years into the future to a conference where G was presenting a beautiful house.

From the front seat audience, an envious peer with 200 projects under his belt confronted G, 'But tell us G, how do you find an ideal client like that?'

'How did I find this client?' G paused.

The envious peer was hitting below the belt. The Crematorium was won through a national design competition[1]. Competitions are rare. It was one of maybe 10 that G had taken part in, and the only one built of the four he had won. It had taken two years to build, and it had been standing for four years, steadily consuming bodies at the rate of 10,000 a year, until one day, a worker in a diamond factory died and was brought to this charity run Crematorium, accompanied by the benevolent Client himself.

'It took 10 years, 10 competitions, four wins, one built, an architect without Soul, another without Spirit and at least a person close to the client to lose his life. But all this is still not enough…' G took a deep breath and continued, '…my number readily available with the Registrar of Death!'

---

1. *Architecture Design Competition, which gives architects the chance to be recognised and win public project commissions.*

Let's move back to the chamber of the Registrar of Death, the one who had called on that overcast, pecked and turbid day.

'Sir, there is a request to call you. Shall I pass?'

'Sure. Pass on.'

The registrar handed the phone to the person waiting next to him.

'This is PS. I like your Crematorium. Would you create a house for us to live in?'

'Sure! We do homes too!'

After the house, PS and G made a few buildings together as client and architect. Instead of till-death-do-us-part, death got them together.

Handle in Hand, Hand in All

G had just finished the Blood Building[1] in the Beloved-city-of-A-Bad. After many years, he was travelling back to the Land-of-Pasta-and-Wine and met a friend from his early days, who now shared his office space with a well-known Italian product designer. Upon introduction, G's eyes scanned the drawing of a door handle and its sample lying on his board. He didn't want to let go of the opportunity: it was an appropriate time to boast.

'We have also designed and made a door handle,' said G, holding a glass of wine in one hand.

'*Bello*[2]! That's nice! You are doing it in your country?' said the surprised Italian.

On seeing the continued interest of the Italian, G took it further, 'Yeah, and in our design, you don't see any screw!' He pointed at a tiny one visible in the designers' sample.

'*Vero*[3]?' The Italian stopped working, 'I haven't come across a handle where there are no screws on the outside. That's magic!'

'Do come visit us!' G was now at his sardonic best.

'*Certo Caro*[4]! I have to come! Always wanted to see the Indian

---

1. *Blood collection and processing plant.*
2. *Beautiful in Italian.*
3. *True in Italian.*
4. *Sure dear in Italian.*

rope trick[5]. And now this handle!'

Bloated G was back in the Beloved-city-of-A-Bad, ready to reap the benefits of his Blood Building, his first large building. And why wouldn't he? It had been a dream project for him. Here he had the liberty to custom design everything to his heart's content. In order to cut costs, everything was designed in-house and fabricated locally. Donor chairs to blood shakers, water coolers to doors, down to even the door handles! A perfect showcase for future clients.

Way back, when I was once in G's Hilly-Home-Town, I saw how his father and younger brother moiled to dismantle and reassemble their antique motorcycle, while G observed casually from a distance, asking complex questions and disturbing them. As his mother cooked delicious chola bhatura[6], *his sister- the youngest of the siblings, told me that in all their growing up years, their mother was the one who toiled to keep the house going with frugal means, albeit high aspirations. She also confided that G rarely greased his hands, only soiled himself mentally. So much so, during his school days, he dreamt of designing future cars and his only aim was to join the product design course at the most premier design institute. Until one day...*

He came across an article written by an esteemed professor from the institute, who had carried out extensive research on his subject of transportation design. However, the title of the article, 'The New Bullock Cart Design,' was enough to put an abrupt end to G's pursuit of a flying career in future car design, and he joined the more rooted architecture course instead. Product design remained his unrequited love[+], whom he could not marry because of the bullish professor, and mechanical instincts that remain coiled up, burst out occasionally through his buildings. The Blood Building had given him ample opportunity to flirt with his first love.

+   *Refer to the story, 'Riding the Curve,' page 159*
5. *Often called the 'world's greatest conjuring trick,' it is a mythical illusion in which a boy climbs a rope rising into the air without any means of support.*
6. *Delicacy in Northern India. Consists of a white chickpea curry paired with deep-fried flatbread made from refined flour.*

Let's go back and check how bloated G was performing upon his return. Indeed, he was waiting for his lucky chance to flirt again.

The phone rang.

'Hello! I am calling from the Blood Building.'

'A new project!' thought G and took the phone in positive anticipation. 'Hello! How is the collection going?'

'Good but...'

G couldn't wait to tell how well received the screwless handle was. 'You know? Even the Italians are talking…'

'…Can you please come?'

'Of course. Will plan in the next few days.'

'It's urgent! I am stuck.'

'Oh! Knew the AC would be a problem!' G was quick to assume.

'Sir, please. Handle!'

'Sure! I'll call the AC vendor immediately …'

'Not AC, Sir! The door handle…'

'You noticed? It's nice, no?' G was still bloated.

'It has come off!'

'Keep it safe, I'll talk to the fabricator!'

'It's in my hand…'

'Oh! It should not have come out. Let me also pull out the drawing in the meantime and check.'

'How do I come out?'

'Come out of where? Are you not at the Blood Building?'

'I'm stuck inside the toilet, Sir!'

That handle in hand left a deep hole in G's passion for his first love and severely punctured his bloated ego. He vowed never to share his screw and love exploits with the Italians. However, he continued to relish their pasta and wine.

Additional Reinforcements
🌶

'OUT! OUT. RIGHT. NOW!' screamed the Col. Almost instantly, the driver brought the car to a screeching halt.

This incident is from a visit to a stone mine that a local land broker had suggested as an investment option to the just-retired and cash rich Colonel, who was also a coveted Maha Vir Chakra[1] *hero. They had started their journey together from the Beloved-city-of-A-Bad just an hour earlier and were yet to travel another 200 kilometres.*

The timid local broker had met and parroted greetings to the Col. 'Big pleasure with you Sir Col. Dig Vijay Singh[2] Maha Vir Chakra Sir!'

'WHAT'S YOUR NAME SON!' the Col. asked politely.

'Sir, me? Das Ran-chod Lal[3] Sir.'

'HOPE YOU'LL NOT LEAVE US HALFWAY MR.RAN-CHOD!' the Col. laughed out loud and tried to make the moment light.

'No way Sir. I with you Sir. Mine is all yours.' The local broker had reassured the Col.

---

1. *Literally 'Great warrior medal' in Hindi. The second highest military decoration in India, awarded for acts of conspicuous gallantry in the presence of the enemy.*
2. Dig Vijay Singh *literally translates to 'the lion who won the battle' in Hindi.*
3. Ranchod *literally translates to 'the one who ran away from the battlefield.' In the* Mahabharata, *it is one of the names given to Lord Krishna, who could appear and disappear at will.* Lal *translates to 'son' in Hindi.*

'I FOUGHT THREE WARS, NOTHING HAPPENED TO ME - WHAT'S A MINE!'

After stories of war and valour, the talk was getting more business-like. 'I get you good deal, Sir. Sir, what is Maha Vir Chakra?'

'DON'T THEY TEACH YOU IN SCHOOL! IT'S A DECORATION FOR BRAVERY!'

'Sorry Sir! Chakra! Society! Lot respect Sir!' the local broker knew he had touched a raw nerve of the man of war.

'HUH! IT'S NOT JUST CHAKRA, IT IS MAHA VIR CHAKRA! YOU SHOULD KNOW BETTER!'

'Understood Sir. But how much you got the Chakra for Sir?'

'OUT! OUT. RIGHT. NOW!' screamed the Col. Almost instantly, the driver brought the car to a screeching halt.

Even before anyone had set foot on it, the mine had exploded.

Das Ran-chod Lal was left deserted in the middle of the Rann[4]. The Col. had meant business even though he hadn't.

Back in the Beloved-city-of-A-Bad, the Col.'s business reputation had preceded him. G was already feeling proud that so early in his career, he was called upon to serve his country when he was chosen by the Col. to be the deserving architect for his house. D-serving probably because the Col. thought that with the same surname as his, when the time came, G would be brave enough to sacrifice himself and not run away from the battleground.

The house would be on a primary urban street, another first for G. Leaving the ground floor for retail, the house was to be

---

4. *Rann of Kutch in Gujarat is one of the largest salt deserts in the world.*

another two floors high. Conceived as a simple cuboid, with curved balconies jutting out from all sides, G had also carried over the idea of four round columns[5] marking the central living space, a hangover from his own house design coming up in those days. All was going smooth and fast. The slab[6] over the basement had already been cast over the quartet of columns, but these were found missing in the ground floor drawings received from G's structural engineer father, fondly called PapaG[+].

'You missed those four round columns? Good I noticed!' G reproached his father.

'I didn't miss. We don't need them; the walls are good enough to carry your building load.' PapaG was always one up.

'You didn't tell me they were not needed? They are already cast in the basement.'

'You like those useless round columns in the middle of your rooms, no? I thought they were for decoration only.'

'Architects don't do anything just for decoration, but you engineers will never understand…' G paused for a while, '…let them continue up further. How can I tell the Col. we cast those columns just for fun?'

'Okay. I still have to provide minimum reinforcement[7] as per the code[8].' PapaG cautioned.

Without carrying any load, the happy columns and Col. silently continued their journey up with the house. Those round lofty columns had almost reached the rooftop which would cover

---

+   *Refer to the story, 'Coronation and Sacrifice,' page 51*
5.   *Elements to carry load vertically and transmit them to the foundation.*
6.   *The horizontal structural plane that forms the floor and ceiling.*
7.   *Steel bars used to take the tension in concrete structures. Together with concrete called Reinforcement Cement Concrete or RCC.*
8.   *Standard codes that provide the guidelines and standards for the design and analysis of structures.*

a double height living space at the centre of the house. G was undecided on the final shape of the roof. The incomplete drawing was still stuck on the drawing board, waiting only for his moment of creative spurt.

It was time for another late evening face-off with the Col. These sessions were always highly spirited.

'I LIKE THE HOUSE, EVERYTHING IS SORTED!' Col. was in his usual happy mood.

'You can easily retire here in the Beloved-city-of-A-Bad, no need to go anywhere else.' Perhaps stationing Col. in the dry city[9] suited G the most, for it could serve as his cheap source for high spirits for long[+].

'I WILL MISS SWIMMING! WISH THERE WAS A POOL WITH MY BAR!'

In our Beloved-dry-city-of-A-Bad, there is no bar on bar for the army, but for us lesser mortals, a bar can lead to one behind bars.

Water…? Bodies…? Amphibian G always loved them.

'Oh! Wish you had told me before. There is no space left on the ground and there is no privacy either. Too late, Col.!' Realising the missed opportunity, G became melancholic.

'HIGH ON THE ROOF SON, NOT ON THE GROUND!' The floating Col. gave a spirited glance.

'Pool on the terrace? Not a joke, Col. You need heavy foundations; your house is almost complete.'

Even in high spirits, G was still grounded, but the floating Col.

+ *Refer to the story, 'Who Slept in His Bed?' page 63*
9. *There is a strict liquor prohibition for all domiciles in Gujarat. This does not apply to army personnel or those visiting from outside the state.*

was getting a bit too imaginative for G's comfort, and then came the bombshell.

'I HAVE FOUGHT THREE WARS, NOTHING HAPPENED TO ME - WHAT'S A POOL!'

One couldn't argue with Col.'s logic. Let me call it Colo-nel-Logic for now.

'Okay Col. I must leave now!' G was worried. If he got too late, Col. may forget to offer him the usual crate of beer, leave too early, and he may not be spirited enough to offer the parting gift.

'WAIT! LET ME GET YOU SOME BEER!'

G patted himself on the back secretly for his immaculate Govinda[+] timing.

'DO THINK ABOUT THE POOL, G!' Reminded the Col. and ordered an orderly to hand over a crate of beer.

'Sure, Col.' Balancing 50,000 litres of water high up on the roof without foundations was next to impossible. Moreover, G's dizzy mind was now occupied with liquids more volatile than water. How to balance the 5 litres of beer on the curvy fuel tank of his *Bullet*[10], that too in full public view. All G had as his inspiration was Murphy's Law: anything good in life is either illegal, immoral or fattening. G was ticking all the boxes that night.

Next morning at the M-Ass-Studio, G looked at the incomplete roof in the sectional drawing pinned on the board. He took a pencil and in one sweeping action, like that of the sword of a samurai, drew the roof shaped like a saucer. This would be the pool. It fitted beautifully. The newly added curve was projecting out from both sides of the cuboidal house, complementing the protruding curved balconies below. But how

---

+   Refer to the story, 'Riding the Curve,' page 159
10. Royal Enfield Bullet 350. *Known for its macho association, this street bike from 1932 is the longest running motorcycle in continuous production worldwide.*

to support the gigantic volume of water three floors high? His hungover mind went round in circles. The yet purportless quartet of round columns on the drawing were staring back at him. Those columns were found to be just enough to carry the extra load of the pool. PapaG's gift had come in handy. Here, Function had followed Form[11] all the way up, and the pool was finally going to be cast supported only on those four columns.

The construction site was like a warfront, and Col. always felt at home there. He would always preset the time for concrete casting. Come what may, it would never change. It was indiscriminate firing from then on.

'STOP WORK! START CASTING NOW!' Col. gave the order.

'Wait Col. They are still tying the reinforcement bars!' G tried his best to make Col. see reason.

'THEY SHOULD HAVE FINISHED BY NOW. WE CAN'T WAIT!' Col. was adamant.

'Let them tie the bars properly. The slab will fall.'

'I HAVE FOUGHT THREE WARS, NOTHING HAPPENED TO ME - WHAT'S A SLAB!'

The sum total of all Gin-O-Logi[+] would still not be enough to beat this one Colo-nel-Logic. During the entire casting process, the Col. would stand there and then, lo and behold, participate by throwing waste cut pieces of the reinforcement bars randomly into the just laid wet concrete.

'Col.! What are you doing? Someone will get hurt!' G tried to intervene.

+   *Refer to the story, 'The Old Monk Who Bought Gin-O-Logi,' page 15*
11. *'Form follows function' was first used by Louis Sullivan. Considered the driving principle of modern architecture, it states that the shape of a building or object should primarily relate to its intended function or purpose.*

'ADDITIONAL REINFORCEMENTS!' Col. gave his war cry.

'What? First, you didn't let them tie the steel, and now you are making the concrete weak...'

'NO G, I AM ONLY MAKING THE SLAB STRONGER!'

Additional reinforcements for Col. were exactly those. Additional Reinforcements[12]!

The curved slab on the four columns was a sight to behold. With the water filled to the brim, the Col. got his private bar and pool on the terrace. Everyone was happy and satisfied. Now only the finishing works were remaining.

A few days later, G was passing by the house and thought of making a quick visit. It wasn't a scheduled stop. He was walking and looking up at the curved bottom of the pool slab in self-admiration. What he saw next completely shook the earth beneath him. It was a vision of Kalidasa[13], only 100 times more catastrophic.

'COL.!!!!' shouted the shell-shocked G, once he found his voice. 'STOP HIM AT ONCE!'

Col. was standing right there and directing a labourer, who was sitting just under the pool, comfortably cross-legged around the round column and cutting the column patiently with a hacksaw. He was already halfway through. Freshly cut bars were shining bright.

'OH! A WATER PIPE WAS FOULING WITH IT, IT'S JUST A COLUMN!' Col. was his usual confident self.

---

12. *Personnel or equipment sent to support military action.*
13. *A classical Sanskrit author, often considered ancient India's greatest playwright and dramatist. Legend says he was sitting on a branch of a tree, trying to saw it off. He was, however, sitting on the wrong end of the branch, so when he finally sawed through the branch, down he tumbled!*

'One way or the other, you are hell-bent on bringing this building down!' G was now genuinely worried.

'I HAVE FOUGHT THREE WARS, NOTHING HAPPENED TO ME - WHAT'S A BUILDING!'

The bars had to be rewelded and concrete was applied over. Still, it was patchwork, not like the original. Anyway, Col. went on to live there happily with his family.

A few years later, there was a devastating earthquake. Many buildings came crashing down. There was talk of a building in Col.'s locality that had fallen because there was a pool on the terrace. This would be the end of both, the retired Col. as well as G's career, which had only just been launched. G couldn't muster up enough courage to even go check on it and nudged PapaG instead. There were lesser chances of a senior citizen being taken POW[14]. PapaG was confident in his calculations but had no clue of Col.'s fiddling with them. However, the building and curved pool were up and standing when he went there. He was welcomed and greeted warmly by the Col.

PapaG asked if everything was alright.

'NOT EVEN A CRACK; SOLID LIKE ME!'

'Thank God.' PapaG was relieved.

'I MADE THE BUILDING STRONG. REMEMBER THOSE ADDITIONAL REINFORCEMENTS?'

'My son told me.' PapaG resisted the urge to overrule Colo-nel-Logic and continued, 'Lots of buildings have fallen down.'

'I HAVE FOUGHT THREE WARS, NOTHING HAPPENED TO ME - WHAT'S AN EARTHQUAKE!'

---

14. *Prisoner of War.*

Epilogue:

The book had just gone for review. We were in the middle of the second wave of Covid-19 and another nationwide lockdown. It had been a clean 20 years since the earthquake. There was an unexpected call from the Col. with whom there had been no contact for years. 'BETA[15]! HOW ARE YOU DOING! HOPE FAMILY IS SAFE!'

'So nice of you to call Col. We are good and getting vaccinated soon. How about you?'

'I HAVE FOUGHT THREE WARS, NOTHING HAPPENED TO ME - WHAT'S A VIRUS!'

---

15. *Son, in Hindi.*

Wit •ness to Mat•Haroo (मत•हारो) Spirit

Coronation and Sacrifice

While his peers chased girls and headbanged to Rock, G toiled to get the windows in his drawing aligned to hill views. His only consolation was that, as a student of architecture, he was getting a head start to build even before he had the licence to practice.

G's family was not new to building, and he was probably destined to play with brick and mortar. G's Great Grandfather, 3G, was a respected designer in the colonial era, whose hand-drafted drawings were salvaged and later put up in M-Ass-Studio: a true testimony to the family lineage. G's father, *Papaji*[1] or simply PapaG, is a simple man of humble beginnings. Trained in structural design, he believed that architecture was just a perspective[2] away. G couldn't shrug off this legacy and soon headed to the School[3], in the Beloved-city-of-A-Bad to set his own perspective right.

Years later, when I trained under G, I appreciated how he skilfully battled to convince the world of his design exploits. Of course, like everyone else, I also thought this skill must have come in his genes, till he described to me how imaginatively his father had coroneted him way back in his student days. It goes like this…

Their house was due to come up when G was still in the third

---

1. *Father in Hindi. Ji is a suffix used at the end of the name as a sign of respect. G's father was fondly called* Papaji *by all those around him.*
2. *Perspective is a method of realistic 3-dimensional drawing, which is part of the architecture curriculum but not of engineering.*
3. *G's alma mater.*

year of his five year architecture course. In those pre-email, pre-mobile, perpetually broke days, communication with the family was only when he went home, once every six months; a trunk call[4] or telegram was meant for grave matters only - funerals or weddings. During one such summer vacation, both father and son competed for their versions of a dream family house. After two months of agonising discussions, with the family mostly voting for G's ideas against PapaG's, most decisions were finally firmed up. The naive student ideas included a house in a perfect grid, overlooking double height volumes and split levels with continuity of spaces. But most importantly, since the site was on a slope in his Hilly-Home-Town, it was about capturing the views of the hills through the windows.

While PapaG waited for the home loan to be sanctioned, G came back to the Beloved-city-of-A-Bad for another semester. Having painstakingly prepared GFC[5] drawings by putting in extra hours, he was extremely delighted about getting a building to boast of. With blueprints[6] rolled and ready, he waited anxiously. No letters came, nor was his design called for.

Months passed and it was time to go home for another semester break. On arrival, he inquired about the loan, but instead PapaG took him to the site of the new house. The loan had indeed been sanctioned, the ground long broken, the house already half built. No, not as per his design, but only on the verbal instructions given by the seasoned PapaG. It was now G's turn to bang his head in vain.

One by one, G tore his drawings as painstakingly as he had

---

4. *When private phones were not common, long-distance or 'trunk' calls were facilitated by an operator at the telephone exchange. Another form of communication across cities was the telegram service – a system of delivering short messages through dedicated telegraph offices, and this redundant service was officially abolished on 14th July 2013, in India.*
5. *Good for Construction. Detailed drawings are stamped as GFC when sent for execution on site.*
6. *A reproduction print of a building drawing. All architects' drawings were issued in this form using ammonia, before the advent of electronic printers.*

made them. PapaG consoled him, in all innocence, that all ideas were still G's. Two rooms were literally joined length to length without the designed level difference in between, making it look like a tunnel! 'You wanted split levels, no? I managed it without those useless steps in between.'

The overlooking space in the double height volume was through a mere 4 x 3 foot window in a 20 foot high wall; a window, replete with a grill and a mosquito net. 'See, you can look down and talk, exactly how you wanted!'

There was no alignment, no proportion and no evidence of a grid whatsoever. 'Grid is visible on paper only, so I did not bother to follow.' PapaG rubbed reason to the wound.

This mental interpretation had made the design genetically mutated; it remained neither G's nor PapaG's. The house was born challenged, both structurally and architecturally. It was a case of an engineer reading an architect's mind instead of his drawings, and a father sacrificing his instincts for the sake of his son.

As if it was not enough, his father continued the guided tour of the house, and took G to the terrace and proclaimed, 'What was all the fuss about aligning views to windows? Look here, only views All around!'

He wished he had not chased views and followed his peers instead. Two years went by. Distraught G was now in his supposedly last semester of thesis[7].

Two semesters in and G had still not finished his thesis[+]! He got a call to attend the biennial, three day *Akhand Paath*[8] at home. G

+   *Refer to the story, 'Wet Love,' page 105*
7. *A dissertation that presents a student's research and is a prerequisite for a professional degree. Though meant for the semester of six months, students at the School of Architecture commonly take up to two years to complete it, and some even took 15.*
8. *The continuous and uninterrupted recitation of the* Guru Granth Sahib, *the sacred scripture of the Sikh religion.*

joined on the second day. No one could miss it, as his most pious grandfather, let's call him 2G, was still alive.

At the closing of the ceremony, amidst 150 attendees, the high priest announced, 'With the blessings of the Lord Almighty, you all will be pleased to know that G, son of PapaG, grandson of 2G and great grandson of 3G, has decided to walk in the footsteps of his father and forefathers. This very *ardas*[9] is in commemoration of him becoming a certified architect!'

G was shocked. Blasphemy! That too, in the name of the Almighty? He had not completed his studies; he was not an architect yet.

'*Puttar*[10] please come forward and accept the Gurus blessings!' announced the head priest even before G could gasp for breath.

What could he do? People had started congratulating him. His father was showing off the mutant house to everyone as G's first baby. He had ascended to be the next 'architect' of the family. It was his coronation in the presence of everyone.

PapaG had lied to the community, but to God too? G was furious, but his furore was hidden under a thick garland that the priest had put around his neck. Later, he blew up, 'What was that nonsense? I am not an architect yet. This is not even my house. Why do this to me?'

'It was high time. Anyway, you wanted to become an architect before you actually became one.' PapaG was always one up.

That was the story of his coronation to the throne, but not without the sacrifice of his first project.

G came back to the Beloved-city-of-A-Bad to continue his thesis. From now on, he would have to fend for himself, have to find himself and most importantly, fund himself.

---

9. *Sikh prayer performed before undertaking or after completing a significant task.*
10. *Son in Punjabi.*

Sleepless Nights

Barely had he started to get some sleep…

A shattering sound pierced through his bedroom in the middle of the night. He woke up with a scream: this was not the first time his sleep was disturbed. Let me start from the very beginning.

Only a few months had passed since Client D had moved into the newly built house. But it was a house without the front door! No front door? How could one sleep peacefully inside? That too a diamantaire. The delay in the arrival of the main door can be attributed to G only; he had proposed an idea that would become another big ongoing project and would only be completed much after Client D moved in. Anyway, better late than never, the door did arrive a few months later and he began to sleep.

*

Barely had he started to get some sleep...

The air conditioning refused to cool the master bedroom. This was a serious matter and was taken up with G. If the client wasn't able to sleep properly, what good are concepts, proportions and finishes? For G, success is measured by the Post Occupancy Performance of the client.

Immediately, three teams of AC consultants, AC suppliers and AC vendors were attending to the problem, the mandate being that they find the fault, rectify it and convince the client enough that he goes off to sleep. Of course, they were not to sleep either till he did. Consultants insisted their calculations were okay, suppliers sure that the machines were the best in the entire market and vendors showed minute-by-minute on-site readings showing perfect cooling. Still, in order to satisfy Client D, the entire system was replaced with a new one, but the situation wouldn't improve.

Eventually, it was decided that the age-old units from Client D's previous house would be brought here and installed. To everyone's surprise, his sleep was restored. Along with the AC consultants, suppliers and vendors, G also went back to sleep. On rigorous analysis by the best minds in the industry, it was concluded that the new ACs were the silent type that Client D was not comfortable with. Maybe they had a silence that was deafening.

*

Barely had he started to get some sleep...

A shattering sound pierced through his bedroom in the middle of the night. He woke up with a scream; a large piece of stone clad on the wall had fallen off and crashed. If this was not bad enough, it was in the master bedroom! If not a legal case, all ties would be broken at least. G wondered how we would explain that the architect's role was only to choose the stone and recommend the best glue for fixing. On closer inspection, it turned out that the stone itself had gotten sliced with one layer still stuck to the wall.

With the stone glued back and the geological fault fixed, Client D's sleep was restored, but the damage was done. G waited for a moment when he could explain to Client D that he had no control over the shattering incident; there was a long and uncomfortable silence between the two.

Some months later, Client D was blessed with a baby. In

celebration, all would be forgiven. It was finally time for G to fix the fallen bond. He congratulated the couple.

'Remember the stone fell exactly nine months back? Can we now safely assume that we had nothing to do with the fall? It was all your own doing!'

The matter ended peacefully in laughter.

*

Barely had he started to get some sleep...

Client D continued to have sleepless nights...
now on account of the...
newborn.

Wit •ness to Mat•Haroo (मत• हारो) Spirit

ATS: Anti-Terrorist Squad

'PK bol rahein hain[1].'

*Like the intern from the ever-graceful Town-of-*Paan[2]*-and-*Nawabs[3]*, whose initials were PK[+] and would answer the phone in the soberest of manners, each character who has been with G over the years has left a mark distinct from the other. It could be an anecdote or an episode, and if nothing else, then a misdeed indeed. Having seen G's transition from his thumping* Bullet[4] *to the raging* Bull[5]*, I would say that there are a few memorable constants and variables at the M-Ass-Studio that have cast deep dents in his otherwise clear head and well-guarded heart.*

One of his earliest team members, L, came as an inheritance from the previous landowner along with the studio itself and continued long after. L was essentially an office boy, and even after so many years of being gone, G is still discovering his hidden talents. Like the famed Pied Piper, he had this inherent ability to successfully drown rats caught overnight in the M-Ass-Studio into the River-by-the-Ashram below. He was known to be a devout of God Nagadeva[6]. By mistake, G once opened L's

---

+   *Refer to the story, 'MUAH!!!' page 83*
1. *'I am drunk and speaking,' when pronounced in Hindi. Long before the Hindi movie* PK *starring Aamir Khan was released.*
2. *Mouth freshener of betel nut and slaked lime wrapped in a leaf. It leaves a red stain in the mouth that one has to spit out.*
3. *Semi-autonomous rulers of Mughal India, known for their polite language.*
4. Royal Enfield Bullet 350. *Known for its macho association, this street bike from 1932 is the longest running motorcycle in continuous production worldwide.*
5. *A sports car with a raging bull as its emblem.*
6. *Snake God*

private cupboard while looking for his nail cutter at the M-Ass-Studio, and bit his nail finding a picture of Ayrton Senna[7] stuck amongst his *Naga* Gods. With a huge data bank of phone numbers, account details and location maps at his fingertips, he was the equivalent of the browser *Google* and gossip-carrier *WhatsApp* in those days. He would recall anything even before the hat was dropped but could also draw a blank at the most critical of times. His most intelligent skill, however, was to never show curiosity about anything related to drawing work, for in his aloofness with all things architectural, he had understood the true value of freedom and happiness!

While L was sharpening his multitasking skills, a young graduate walked in to learn the art of design from G. She was hardworking and sincere, and seemed to belong. With her learning tempo high and the climate ripe in that place and time, a relationship that went way beyond art and learning was firmly cast in their hearts; she married G, and the Constant K[+] was added to his life.

There is a continuous flow of interns who come for a few months and sometimes get trapped for longer, oh so willingly. I can talk a bit about these interns in G's life, as I myself was the first one, and even after 30 years, it seems to me that I have never left. Whether interns end up learning or not is not in my scope to comment, but they certainly bring an undercurrent to make the Pool[8] of people shimmer rather than reflect.

In the last year of the first decade of the millennium, a completely new set of interns flocked in all the way from the distant South. I would call them ATS, but not directly, for I am under their constant radar too; well, the ATS here is not our Anti-Terrorist Squad but more of Anytime Trouble Shooters, just to clarify to them once and for all. Actually, ATS is an acronym derived from

---

+   *Refer to the story, 'Wet Love,' page 105*
7.   *Widely regarded as one of the greatest Formula 1 drivers, who had passed away earlier.*
8.   *The new Matharoo Associates' Studio in Ahmedabad that is christened 'Pool' and includes a 25 metre swimming pool along the entire length of the working space.*

ATS: Anti-Terrorist Squad

their names. They quickly learnt the tricks of the trade with their endless capacities, and as G kept raising the bar, they leapt up and delivered. While they went beyond critique to correct and discipline him, he continued to enjoy the joyful pain of his own reformation. Slowly, they took charge from him, so much so that even his clients started to feel the heat.

A had a mind of her own. She genuinely believed that erotica was engraved on temple walls to attract common people towards the religion. With her great clarity and confidence, she brought out design concepts in mesmerising watercolours with aplomb, taking over from where G had left[+]. Extremely articulate in English and trying to cultivate the same proficiency in Hindi, instead of *bindaas*[9], she once confidently referred to a lady client as *bewafaa*[10].

T, the lone survivor, is always alert and tracking G's wayward interests[++]. She even got a whiff of our secret book production and the associated time loss, while she herself was seriously packaging a monograph on the M-Ass-Studio practice. G has been sufficiently warned that his time could be better spent checking plumbing and drainage drawings than laughing out loud with his friends while reading and editing stories. So much so that G had to resort to toilet-texting[+++] to complete our book. She is extremely organised and great at multitasking, but always has a single-minded focus on the task at hand. Once when she couldn't find her phone and in panic started calling her friends and family, it took some time before they could explain to her that she couldn't find her phone because it's the one she's calling them from.

S had an air of sweet authority to her. For hours together, she would patiently propose G's crazy ideas to clients, which they

---

+   *Refer to the story, 'Ghost Behind the Disappearing Walls,' page 89*
++   *Refer to the story, 'Yearning for Love,' page 117*
+++ *Refer to the story, 'A Piece of Blue Putridity,' page 165*
9.   *Free-spirited in Hindi.*
10. *Unfaithful to a lover or spouse in Hindi.*

then couldn't refuse. As a perfectionist, she showed dedication very early on. Once when an image was to go for publication, the SOP[11] as per G-System Code 303 was to straighten-lighten-brighten. She coolly violated the code by cleaning up and making an accidentally captured stray piglet in the picture look pinker instead of just trimming it out. With this double loyalty towards pigs and G, he was bowled twice over!

ATS had to be busted most evenings by literally pulling the plugs, or they would never shut shop. Not only did they handle any type of task and tempers of tough clients, they also sorted G's self-created erratic travel schedules and routine tantrums. They made everything look done and dusted. Spoilt with this treatment by the squad, G became almost invisible from the scene of action and added F1 viewing with his siesta.

Being a continuing witness to the ATS phenomenon, I recall a movie where the three lady protagonists keep delivering tasks assigned to them by an invisible boss, and it wouldn't be wrong to call the ATS G's Angels. I made the mistake of hesitantly disclosing their newfound identities to them. With an I-could-care-less look, they went on to accomplish his next....... MAD mission.

---

11. *Standard Operating Procedure.*

Who Slept in His Bed?

Once upon a time, G was young, single and lived happily. One fine day, he had an unexpected visitor, expected to live with G, at least temporarily if not forever, as decided by both their families.

Those were the days when G was being shunted out of his rented accommodations every 11 months; as beyond one year, the laws would turn slightly in favour of the tenant. He had to shift seven homes trying to find a foothold in his Beloved-city-of-A-Bad, till he settled in his own[+]. He was in his third rented place when the unexpected visitor knocked on the door.

The living room in this apartment had been converted into a makeshift studio with two large drafting tables tucked in the corners. I was privileged to be part of this stage of G's career, working as an intern along with a draftsperson D-Man[++].

The only other room was small and almost fully occupied by his self-designed double bed with a storage box underneath, which he carried from one rented apartment to another. The solitary window from this bedroom opened into a corridor outside, so it remained perpetually closed. Over time, the ceiling was slowly getting covered with cobwebs. In the cosy bedroom, one could see the whites of the plaster disappearing into thick shades of grey. It's only a matter of a few months, why bother cleaning, G would reason, looking up at it. This is where he would take his short nap after lunch - which we all ate together - while D-Man

+   *Refer to the story, 'Indecent Proposal?' page 99*
++ *Refer to the story, 'Lost Era of the Blu Printagosaurus,' page 75*

and I would head back to our tables to work.

G once rode off for a meeting somewhere far, only to find himself back in the home studio, wondering if he had somewhere to go. We kept imagining what turns he must have taken subconsciously that brought him back to the same place where he started, and it turns out it was only his sixth sense. As when he returned, the main door was ajar and D-Man and I were missing in action. In a turn of events, we were found sound asleep on the only bed that was available, while spiders continued to spin right above. As they say, people who stay in glass houses should not throw stones at others; he had no choice but to keep mum. He stayed calm. In his calmness, however, there was a firm resolve: never to mix his house and studio again.

Such was the setting in which arrived the unexpected visitor. To say that G was happy with this family decision may not be entirely true. However, G wasn't entirely droopy either. Wait! There was a bait. The visitor-with-benefits came along with the priciest thing anyone could afford in this Beloved-dry-city-of-A-Bad.

His maternal uncle, a devout Sikh, was ex-army and still possessed an army canteen card. G would maximise the benefits by balancing a crate of beer on the tank of his Bullet[1], *well-honed during the Dig Vijay Singh days[+], while simultaneously tolerating freshly brewed sardar jokes[2] from the Uncle on the pillion. Needless to say, his place became a sought-after hangout; for G when the Uncle wasn't around and for the Uncle when G wasn't. This negotiated game of musical Bed & Beer continued fluidly.*

One day, the Uncle told G that one of his friends wanted their house interior to be designed by him. Though G is wary of clients coming via the family route, work is work. He met the Uncle's friend's family with caution. After pleasantries and ice-breaking,

---

+   *Refer to the story, 'Additional Reinforcements,' page 41*
1.   Royal Enfield Bullet 350. *Known for its macho association, this street bike from 1932 is the longest running motorcycle in continuous production worldwide.*
2.   *A class of ethnic jokes based on stereotypes where the* Sardar *or male adult Sikh, is shown as naive, inept or unintelligent.*

the Uncle's friend poured his heart out.

'We had actually selected another architect and were going ahead with him, but then I saw your house.'

'Which one? I have hardly done any!' G was feeling disoriented.

'The office that you live in.'

'That rented ramshackle place? It's just for 11 months. Not even my design. What did you see in it?'

'Your bedroom...'

'What...?' G was disoriented and lost.

'It made me nostalgic about my happy bachelor days!'

'Sorry my place is messy.' G was now disoriented, lost and also embarrassed.

'No No No No! Those cobwebs reminded me of my ceiling from when I was young!' clarified the Uncle's nostalgic friend and now G's client.

The next day, when G broke the news, I teased him. 'Spiders trapping clients for an architect? Another first for you!'

G didn't sleep that afternoon, for he still could not connect the dots. Lost in thought, he lay in bed looking at the ceiling full of cobwebs.

That evening, I poked him a bit deeper. 'I understand your Uncle brought his friend home, but how did his eyes meet the ceiling in your bedroom?' It hit him straight in his soft spot.

'You think he also slept on my bed?'

Wit •ness to Mat •Haroo (मत• हारो) Spirit

Love for Wives and Guns

Gun shooting was a common hobby between the two of them.

'Whenever abroad, I go to a range to try out different guns!'

'Oh really? I also never miss a chance whenever I'm in the U.S. of A.' G was quick to add.

Vada pav[1] breaks, the Big Boss[2] *studio on the way and driving six hours in confinement to and from the site, was bringing out their true characters. Visits would be interesting and beneficial, thought G, although a bit prematurely.*

Leaving the Megapolis-on-an-Island behind, Client C had bought a piece of land in a lush green valley with a rivulet flowing through. The sloping terrain kissed a perennial river[+] at the bottom end, and it was one of the most scenic sites that G was endowed with.

'Killer views!' Smiling G could not control his admiration for the site once they reached.

'I checked many properties before laying my hands on this one. You know, I have a 50 foot pole camera[3]? I attach it to my SUV!'

+   *Refer to the story, 'Politics of a Lone Tree,' page 95*
1. *A vegetarian fast-food dish native to the state of Maharashtra; consists of a fried potato and coriander dumpling, placed inside a half sliced bun.*
2. *A popular reality TV show, where contestants are locked in a house for days.*
3. *A remote controlled camera mounted on a telescopic pole to capture images from a bird's eye view.*

said the sharp Client C, whose other hobby was apparently to peek down from the skies long before the invasion of drones.

It was their first visit to the site. One could see the homes of celebrities dotted along the road. Though the arrival to the plot was at the top end of the slope, G wanted to locate the house much lower, almost falling into the water.

'So near, yet so far! You still want to be by the road like the others? Isn't it better bang on the river?'

G had already started designing in his mind. With their targets aligned perfectly, this would finally be the dream project G had been aiming at for some years. After a careful assessment of each other's differing skills, both G and Client C had decided to make the most of this exquisite site and of course, of each other. The game was on.

'I agree, but for my parents, we will have to make the down trail drivable.' Client C was reluctant to be being placed lower, but also not wanting to be left high and dry.

'The easier the access, the more you'll come here. We will make a small track: you won't have to walk.' G tried selling a Cost versus Use mathematical model. 'Look! The entire river is visible here, from under the canopy of trees. This spot will become the living room, your hide site.'

Shot by shot, G scanned the scene. The house was marked.

'Yes. The view is much better here than from the top.' Client C was convinced.

'Let there be only one bedroom; the kids can sleep in the living room whenever they come.' G wanted to show off his approach of saving everywhere.

'Makes sense.' Client C was getting charged. Anything frugal could be sold to him. Seduced by the environs, for G, the size didn't matter.

'We should do barrel piles[4], not a normal foundation. It's fast and doesn't disturb the million-year-old subsoil.' G was very touchy about the virgin site.

'I know an agency, will get it organised.' As always, the client knows it all.

'When you have guests, the hall and the verandah can be combined with the bar and the barbeque area.' G sharpened his focus on frugality.

'We are Js, not non-vegetarian. We don't drink and party!' Nobody could wriggle out of Client C's non-violent grip.

'Great! We will save a lot if we avoid the bar.' G's shot, too, didn't go blank.

J-Kno-Logic and Gin-O-Logi[+] were locked in perfect cross-hairs. G always fears this total agreement and extreme togetherness, which makes it hard to ask for fees later. He dreads this eventual statement coming from overfriendly clients - 'We were both having fun designing. You were drawing and I was paying to get it built.'

G had already stepped half into it; just another step in or pull out of it now. However, the site being far from the Megapolis-on-an-Island, hours together in a car could not be without banter, which was now getting a tad too personal.

The house lineout was ready for G to check. Cement, mixer and labour were waiting. It was now their second visit to the site.

+ *Refer to the story, 'The Old Monk Who Bought Gin-O-Logi,' page 15*
4. *Long pillars that extend downwards into the ground as a foundation, typically used in situations where the top layer of soil is fragile.*

'Don't you have a weekend house?' asked Client C.

Thinking of his Beloved-city-of-A-Bad - flat and dry, in letter and in spirit - G was now on the defensive. 'Ha! I'm not loaded. You think I can afford one? We could barely manage the swimming pool you saw in our studio.'

'I came for the inauguration, is it real?'

'Oh! I missed telling you. The studio doubles up as our weekend house when closed for work. That is where we spend our days and entertain friends.'

'That's nice, and during weekdays, the whole office must be enjoying the water.' added Client C. Both were now firing in unison.

G was happy his reasoning was being appreciated. He continued further, 'The pool is available to all and so, kept maintained as well.'

'Yeah, there are so many maintenance issues when a place is not used. I can't even think of a pool here.'

'You have a full-blown river, why do you need a pool?' G continued pampering Client C with frugality. 'We are also making your house watertight. So hardly any maintenance.'

'That's very important; things should be in working condition when we come here.'

'How many visits a month do you think?' G wanted to determine the required budget based on the usage.

'Count maximum of two rounds a month. Early in life, when we had time, we didn't have the means; now we have the means, and we have run out of time.' Client C didn't seem to be in a mood to retire anytime soon and reasoned further, 'My wife takes the brunt more than me. We reach in the afternoon and she won't be able to relax till the house is set in order…'

'…While you will be handling defunct pumps and fuses, with the staff.' G almost took words away from Client C.

'Next day, we won't be able to leave till the dishes are done.' Client C was calling the shots now.

G added, 'You should take time out and stay here longer.'

'So true! The more she dreads coming, the lesser we'll come.'

'To avoid such issues, we just step out of our dry state. There are old palaces with nice lakes to choose from nearby.'

While dreaming of royalty for himself, G was proposing rough concrete to Client C.

'Sounds great, but isn't it a hole in the pocket?'

'One can do a weekend trip within Rs.30,000 and the best part, you leave dirty dishes behind.' G was now serving another round of Gin-O-Logi.

'And you even bought sports cars with the money you saved. Our priorities are different though.' Client C wanted to gauge how G still manages to drive sports cars.

'Second-hand ones are not that expensive. Even with your modest house budget, you can buy a few of them or choose to make many shooting trips abroad.' Gin-O-Logi was now getting too deadly for Client C.

'So true! That's enough for a whole lifespan.' Client C was now aching for more!

The third trip to the site was in a sports convertible. Client C was taking G for a joyride in his new second-hand acquisition.

'It's fully armed! Six cylinders and straight pipe silencer. You like the firing?' Client C was now revving his new machine.

'Smoking hot!'

'Good thing about second-hand cars is you don't have to declare the price.' Client C had taken G's frugal game one step further.

'Now you can enjoy these drives even more.'

'I bought this and already booked our next family holiday. We are going abroad tomorrow!' Client C smiled, and made a shooting gesture with both his forefingers.

G was happy that Client C was opting for an outdoor lifestyle, just like he had proposed with the new house.

As they reached the site, it was now turn for G's internal combustion chambers to misfire. Within seconds, his happiness was wiped out. It was the moment when the river stood still, leaves didn't flutter and the dust remained settled. On the pristine land, some lumpy sacks of dried cement lay scattered, a few stained tools stayed partly buried in the undergrowth, flies clung onto the long jammed concrete mixer. No movement, no labour, no sign of life.

'What happened here?' Triggered G could barely speak.

'You know G, our entire diamond industry works on the principle that the more you love somebody, the more you spend on diamonds. Your philosophy of loving more by spending less touched my heart.' said Client C, but G was still not getting it.

'I wonder, shouldn't we also leave the dirty dishes behind like you?' said the newly enlightened Client C, point blank.

G was now hit by his own boomerang. Client C had washed his hands off the project and drained G out dry.

Under the canopy, the river was flowing beautifully. The lush green trees were now replete with chirping birds. The little rivulet within the site had transformed into a babbling brook. It was a sight to behold, but sadly, there was no house on site.

Their love for wives and guns had claimed an unsuspecting victim, the innocent house that was to be their...ultimate trophy!

Epilogue:

Among the many calls from past clients during the Covid-19 nationwide lockdown, there was one from Client C.

'Hope all is well!'

'Yes, everyone is working from home. We are living at our studio!'

'The one with the pool? Your weekend house?'

'Yes! The same one.'

'It's good you are isolated and safe. Here, we are easy targets in our apartments. Wish we had not changed our mind and spent these days by the river.'

'Oh! You got rid of your property?'

'Never! It's a catch of a lifetime!'

'Then what is coming in your way?'

'Your ideas on saving!' C wanted to be loud and clear. 'We want the house designed by you, but without you dishing out your dirty philosophy.'

So began the construction and G vowed to keep his Gin-o-Logi to himself.

Lost Era of the Blu Printagosaurus
🌶 🌶 🌶

D-Man[+] couldn't stop his excitement. 'Sir! It's rising! Rising out of my table, Sir!'

Filled with criss-cross lines, G had marked some areas to be blacked out on the drawing of a plan. D-Man went about inking them diligently and mindlessly. After some time, he was shocked to see his own drawing; it was not flat anymore. Lines had become planes, and planes had become solids protruding in and out of the paper, making it look like a 3-dimensional entity. For D-Man, who had been drawing lines as mere lines for so long, sciography[1] was simply pure magic. D-Man had not seen this phenomenon in his six years at the M-Ass-Studio. Little did he know, it was only the beginning of what the future had in store for him.

What happens next requires me to take you down to the lost prehistoric era of a procedure that was unavoidable before the irruption of computers that made it extinct. I am allotting it three Mirchis. Hope you are ready for it.

Who can forget the days of matchmaking chats at a chai-galla[2] *over a* cutting[3], *the joy of conservatively clicking a film roll of only 36 frames[4]*

+   *Refer to the story, 'Who Slept in His Bed?' page 63*
1. *A branch of science dealing with the projection of shadows, giving the drawing a 3-dimensional and realistic appearance.*
2. *Roadside tea-stall in Hindi.*
3. *Half a cup of tea in colloquial Gujarati lingo.*
4. *The maximum number of photographs possible on a single roll of film in an analogue camera, before the advent of digital technology.*

to tell the whole story or placing car speakers on matkas[5] for that Bose[6] effect? Limited resources coupled with ample constraints often bring out the best in people's lives.

Pre-computer days were tactile and humane. The drawing board was a sacred zone - each of them was unique, with tools assimilated and laid out differently. Further, intimate engagement happened through innumerable doodles and scribbles dotting the base sheet, giving a sneak peek into one's personal life. There was a standard decorum of guarding and protecting it, covering it with dry soft cloth and clean paper, as if putting the sheet to bed, before calling it a day. Utmost care was taken not to render it with sepia rings of tea and other culinary exploits of the day. To clear the frivolous freckles and marks, the humble leftover bread, that too without butter, was the only edible allowed on the board, to be rubbed on the drawing for a cleansing ritual.

Each drawing was a distilled process to arrive at a few meaningful lines and had a personality of its own. Even though drawn by the same set of tools on classic Gateway tracing[7], one could still make out whose drawing it was just by the intensity of how the lines met, crossed and ended. There were punters of perfection like D-Man, those who could draw to half a millimetre precision. I am sure they saw through their minds and not their eyes, like Arjuna[8].

The rarest of rare dexterities was the art of stencilling[9]. In order to get the perfect rhythm of spacing strokes and alignment, one had to have complete control of hand, breath and mind, like a true yogi. While D-Man had elevated himself to such levels of speed that he could almost

---

5. Earthen pots normally used to cool and store water in Hindi.
6. A premium brand of speakers, often referred to while describing good bass.
7. A translucent paper often used for hand drafting building drawings before the advent of computer-generated drawings. Gateway is the brand name used as a generic term.
8. One of the five Pandavas in the Mahabharata. During the swayamvara, the Indian practice of a girl selecting her husband from a group of suitors, often based on a skill or power challenge. Arjuna was able to pierce the eye of a revolving fish to win the hand of Princess Draupadi as his wife.
9. Letter stencils of various sizes and fonts used by designers and draftsmen as a way to add consistent and precise lettering to drawings, before the advent of computer-generated ones.

use it as handwriting, there remain a few like me who believe it was an act of acute torture, and always hoped that labour laws apply to this extreme human rights violation.

Any further correction on the tracing sheet would be a few careful trims and cuts, precise blade shaves and patches stitched perfectly like an immaculate surgical procedure. As projects progressed with many a correction, the tracings matured with age too. Dog-ears and yellowing, wrinkles and creases caused by casual slips, bruises and stains from manhandling - all telling a tale of their own.

This laborious inking and stencilling on tracing sheets would ensure our thoughts were cross-checked before reproduction. The prehistoric times of G's Great Grandfather, 3G$^+$, was of the Blu Printagosaurus[10]. However, it was now an extinct species and we were surviving in the reproduction era of its true-blue descendant, the Ammonogosaurus[11].

Everything was about smell, touch and feel. Everyone had tears doing this act, neither crocodile nor emotional, only ammonia! It was an intense action of rolling the drawing on a Star Wars[12] *looking blue light and dashing to shove the drawing in that lonely empty box[13], hung in a dark remote corner of the studio. Out came a blue imprint of lines that one had slogged on for days. As these drawings aged on site, they metamorphosed into innumerable blues. Not moody, but of serious commitment. So even after all the high-tech inkjet, laser, multicolour printing of today, the drawing that goes to site from the M-Ass-Studio is still a true blue Ammonogosaurus. It is like liquid currency, not to be printed casually by any copier!*

I got a bit carried away. Those times were such.

+ *Refer to the story, 'Coronation and Sacrifice,' page 51*

10. *Traditional blueprint with white lines on a blue background, in practice until the 70s. The reproduction process used an ammonia solution and involved the cumbersome sun-drying of the paper.*

11. *The new form of blueprint with blue lines on a white background. This faster reproduction process used gaseous ammonia.*

12. *Sci-fi fantasy film series created in 1977.*

13. *A small wooden chamber where reproductions of the* Gateway *drawing on paper are exposed to ammonia gas, developing blueprint copies.*

Let's go back to the new drawing presently on D-Man's board.

It was a plan for a resort with no two walls parallel, which he was meticulously drafting and the drawing was almost complete. The project was won through an invited design competition[14]. G was happy to have a rocky riverfront site.

Looking at the design concept sketch, the Client had already exclaimed, 'I have never seen a building rising out of water, like a rock. Except in my dreams, maybe.'

Hearing this, G must have felt like Howard Roark[15]- let's call him H. The 'rock rising out of water' idea had a problem though, we only realised later: regional regulations demanded the building be a minimum 100 feet away from the river edge.

'Don't let 100 feet of rock shatter your dreams, let's shatter the rocks instead!' Thus spoke H, residing deep inside G.

The Client was convinced enough to acquire a mining licence to blast off the rocks from the 100 foot margin[16] and also use that stone for construction. Even before the dust had settled, it dawned upon G that the building still didn't kiss the river, and the random jagged profiles of both, the river and the resort plinth, were yet longing to meet. What a pity! After months of labour, all drawings hand-drafted and stencilled, blueprints[17] ready to be sent, time ticking. And G? He goes for his meditative nap, leaving H flipping in his grave.

He woke up and declared. 'Flip the drawing!'

---

14. *Architecture Design Competition, which gives architects the chance to be recognised and win public project commissions.*
15. *Howard Roark is the protagonist in Ayn Rand's famous book* The Fountainhead. *He is an architect who battles conventional norms and refuses to compromise with an architectural establishment unwilling to accept innovation.*
16. *Minimum distance from the site boundary that must be maintained without any building, as per local byelaws.*
17. *A reproduction print of a building drawing. All architects' drawings were issued in this form using ammonia, before the advent of electronic printers.*

Thanks to the transparent *Garware*[18] tracing sheet, D-man did it as fast as he heard G.

'Beauty!' The mirrored drawing now perfectly entwined the river profile into a tight hug. Now the building truly seemed like a 'rock rising out of water.'

'Now just blueprint the drawing in reverse and send.' G loved these time-less solutions[+].

Warm and fragrant, the newly hatched test print was laid out. Everything was perfect, until someone pointed out that all the stencilled text, labelling and dimensions had mirrored into a prehistoric script. The sheets would still have to be stencilled all over again, and with just the thought of it, everyone's faces too turned into various scales of blue.

As much as we were relieved at the maximum effect with minimal effort, our blues deepened further. Unlike the more expensive *Gateway*, the writing could not be done on the glossy backside of the cheaper *Garware* sheet, which was now the norm. Grim G's grin had vanished, only to return more confused and hesitant, 'Stencil also in reverse!'

Our blessings had now turned into a curse. A short command, but for D-Man who could think only as straight as he drafted, life mirrored itself completely for the next few days.

Mirrors often create havoc in people's lives, transcending them overnight from being transparent to mirror personalities of themselves. Watching D-Man stencil in reverse, I was sure he'd at least end up becoming a lefty, would ride only on the right side of the road or enter the house opposite his own. A few days later, the blueprints were sent, leaving no marks of this extreme tedious procedure. The following

---

+   *Refer to the story, 'Scape Goat and the Cross-Legged Mummy,' page 151*

18. *A translucent and waterproof plastic sheet with high dimensional stability and tear strength. Being cheaper, it replaced the earlier used* Gateway *sheet. Garware is the brand name used as a generic term.*

morning, D-Man went missing.

No intimation, no message, no phone call. The G-System Code 911 to declare emergency or 'E' had been breached. G kept his cool. The next day, he confronted D-Man. 'D you were E.'

'Yes, Sir. Yes.'

'What happened?'

'Nothing happened. Nothing!'

'Why not inform?'

'I would. What would I?'

'C'mon! Reason for not coming?'

'Sir, reason? No reason, Sir.'

Alas, my fears about D-Man's mirrored state of mind had come true. G reflected on the unreasonable reasonability of the situation, but to still have the last word...'Good excuse! Just don't ever use this again.'

That very day, a revision was added to his G-System Code 911 - Just mention E, give no reason.

So, D-Man would now call up and only say, 'D, Sir. Sir, E.'

'Fu...ine!' G would mutter and swallow the H inside him.

Like the era of the Blu Printagosaurus, the era of the Ammonogosaurus was fading too, replaced by glossy and flashy page 3 characters churned out of printers, where you can't make out one from the other. However, some rare specimens of the species still remain to date, like those found at the M-Ass-Studio.

What happened to D-Man?
D-Man also joined the bandwagon and became A-Man, an ace AutoCAD operator.

The dream project?
Embracing the river, the mossy walls still rise up, but not high enough, like remnants from a bygone era. The resort was abandoned halfway through.

The reason?
While the dreamer Client could acquire a violent mining licence within days, he could not acquire a non-violent licence for liquor sale, in this land of Gandhi.

And what about H?
Deep inside G, he still keeps flipping in his grave occasionally[+].

+ *Refer to the story, 'Can I Hug You?' page 179*

Wit •ness to Mat •Haroo (मत• हारो) Spirit

MUAH!!!

'Snd T in'

It was a usual day at the M-Ass-Studio. G sent an SMS[1] from his push-button mobile phone[2] when the Clients arrived for a meeting. Those were the days of the River-by-the-Ashram, where G still had his glass cabin. Moments later, a junior architect walked in, stood mute and steadfast. After a while, G, paused his conversation with the Clients and turned to her, 'Yes?'

When the confused junior architect didn't reply, G asked, 'Is it urgent?'

'I don't know, you called for me!' said the junior architect, even more confused now.

'No, I didn't.' said G. The junior architect left, completely baffled.

The meeting was coming to an end and tea had not been served yet. Not feeling good about having to remind, G sent another SMS. 'Cn u snd T in quik?'

'I came in no...?' popped in the previously baffled, now irritated junior architect.

---

1. *Short Message Service. Before* WhatsApp *and mobile data became commonplace, a single text message allowed for only 160 characters. Going even one character over this limit, meant being charged double.*

2. *The earliest mobile phones had a set of 12 buttons with an alpha-numeric keypad for dialling and typing, as opposed to the digital touch screens of today.*

'What!!!?' It was G's turn to be confused, baffled and irritated.

'I came but you said you didn't call me!'

And then it struck G. 'Oh! Send *chai*[3] in now.'

Now it was the Clients' turn to be confused and baffled. G clarified, 'We call everyone in the studio by just the first letter of their name. Hers starts with T. Hence the mix-up with Tea.'

The Clients were left amused, not realising their names too would be reduced to a mere sound or a syllable here.

'Is your GHAAV[4] clear? And SCAR still there? Dispatch the set of LAFA[5] to the site engineer!'

I am no stranger to these abnormal-sounding exchanges at the M-Ass-Studio. People new to the studio may think that some alien language is being spoken in some of the last remaining pockets of Earth. Just like their intern PK[+].

We have heard of naming and branding, but designers can make a project of that too. Architect Eisenman[6] named his projects House No.1 or House No.10, reducing them to mere numerical entities. But names in our country can have complex roots in caste, guild or place of origin. They can also be cumbersome when you add a salutation, like Param Pujya Dharma Dhurandhar[7] Sri Sri Ganpateshwar Gurudev *or* PPDDSSGG *in G's words. Moreover, it is a nightmare fitting project titles in limited space on drawing sheets; imagine having to stencil[8]* Corporate House for Beer Bottle Openerwala & Dikras[9] *time*

+   *Refer to the story, 'ATS: Anti-Terrorist Squad,' page 59*
3. *Tea in Hindi.*
4. *Wound in Hindi.*
5. *A slap in Gujarati.*
6. *Peter Eisenman. American architect known for his deconstructive designs.*
7. *A decoration given to learned scholars of the Hindu religion.*
8. *Letter stencils of various sizes and fonts used by designers and draftsmen, as a way to add consistent and precise lettering to drawings, before the advent of computer-generated ones.*
9. *Sons, a word used by the Parsi community.*

and again and being reminded of impending deliverables or pending payments.

Disrobing people of their past baggage and renaming them is a given at M-Ass-Studio, a place where past influence or association doesn't matter. You are de-briefed and baptised after a dip in the Pool[10] and a code is assigned to you, but you can continue to wear your own old genes.

Thus, a new system, let's call it G-System Code UNBOND700 for the sake of simplicity, was evolved to codify titles with convenient parameters like letters in the client's name, the city and type of project, so that at least internally the project could be traced down to its roots. But the rules of the system are not easy; the new word thus formed must have a rhythmic sound and, when expanded, it must have the correct syntax too. Much more difficult than Scrabble[11], as you are given only a limited number of 3 or 4 letters that you can't exchange and must form words that may not exist. The game is as in-tense as it gets, and to top it all, you need to crack the correct name even before the design has a concept. Using them saves repeated typing, stencilling or uttering long names but, I assume, it's also gaining valuable time in their lives for better things.

The name game started with only simple rhyming sounds of letters like PSRS (P...S...R-esidence at City-of-Diamonds) and the second house in the city became DSRS (D...S...R-esidence at City-of-Diamonds). These humble beginnings were, however, very short-lived. The simple act of combining letters started churning out weird sounds as if it were a self-learning programme in some unknown language.

Long before the wedding sagas of HAHK[12], DDLJ[13] and KKHH[14]

---

10. *The new Matharoo Associates' Studio in Ahmedabad that is christened 'Pool' and includes a 25 metre swimming pool along the entire length of the working space.*
11. *A board game where players compete in forming words with lettered tiles on a 225-square board.*
12. *Hindi movie:* Hum Aapke Hain Koun..!
13. *Hindi movie:* Dilwale Dulhania Le Jayenge
14. *Hindi movie:* Kuch Kuch Hota Hai

became a custom in Hindi movies, it was already a well-groomed system at the M-Ass-Studio. Barring a few projects like OVAL, ORDOS and INCOR, which came peti-pack[15] from the clients and bypassed the G-System Code UNBOND700, all others have had to go through rigorous mumbo jumbo.

Even while being extra careful with four letter words, which could get scandalous, some like GHAP, GSAD and GSAL still started sounding like failed government schemes of Gujarat. A few like AAARAA, VOJIS and LOGECO became puzzles of sorts, challenging our own established notions. AALA, SARAS and even RAAG got back the essence of cultural practices. Ones like FHAS, VRAA and GRAA remained just leftovers of deep bowel sounds. Those like KTRA, AAA and LAFA even got violent emotions played out, often with a resulting condition of GHAAV and were even left with a SCAR. Beloved-city-of-A-Bad and without Gandhi? A bit of Gandhigiri also came out through SWA[16], and to quench the dryness of the state, DRAVA[17] is there, of course.

G's students don't feel left out either; they SCREAM[18] at the sounds of CHAMBAL[19] - acronyms for the semester long design tasks given at the School[20]. The height of this phenomenon is that some students even go down to the PITS[21] on his travelling classes.

In RASA, a plain abbreviation of the client's name, project and place turned out to be just that - a medley of various *rasas*[22]. The client loved the name so much that they retained it as the house

---

15. *Unopened in Hindi slang.*
16. *Self in Sanskrit. Mahatma Gandhi had propagated the concept of Swaraj, or self-rule, during the Independence movement.*
17. *Substance in Hindi.*
18. *Project title: SCheme for Regional Employment And Monitoring.*
19. *Project title: Crocodile Habitat And Monitoring, Baths And Laboratories.*
20. *G's alma mater.*
21. *Pan India Travel Studio, academic program of which G is a co-founder member.*
22. *Flavour, sentiment or emotion: regarded as one of the fundamental qualities of classical music, dance and poetry.*

name, of course, free of any royalty. Another named JARS turned out to be a composition of rotating concentric cylindrical walls; yes, you got it right, rotating around each other as if lids on a jar. MOHA went the farthest, becoming an innocent victim of the tragic saga of *Moha Maya*[+].

The names were becoming immortal. It's not a bad idea to have the power of name calling and getting liked or laughed at. Many names evolved to suit the project, but it was uncanny to me how the projects were now evolving to become the given names.

I cautioned G, 'Your buildings are becoming the names you give them. Be careful what you call them before it's too late.'

Years had gone by since T had entered the cabin instead of Tea. Now a frontrunner and lone survivor of the ATS[++] trio, she introduced a new project to the office. A mix of commercial, recreational and residential functions, situated in the far-off City-of-Round-Rocks-and-Pearls.

'What's the natural name turning out to be?' G knew the jumbling time had come.

'Multi Use At Hide-bad.' T proclaimed in earnest.

'MUAH? Okay! Let's go...' He paused, my warning replaying slowly in his head: *Your buildings are becoming the names you give them.* Just in the nick of time, he changed mid-course '...go find another!'

Saving many blushes before it could become basorexia.

+   *Refer to the story, 'Moha Maya,' page 193*
++ *Refer to the story, 'ATS: Anti-Terrorist Squad,' page 59*

Wit •ness to Mat •Haroo (मत• हारो) Spirit

Ghost Behind the Disappearing Walls
🌶️ 🌶️

The building was falling down. The floors were visibly tilting on one side, and its corner was leaning dangerously out of plumb. No one ventured near it; it was only a matter of days before it completely embraced the earth. The just built Corporate Headquarters for the State Finance? Aren't they supposed to be wealthy and stable? A really sad state of affairs, I thought.

But for G, it was sadistic pleasure. Only a few years earlier, M-Ass-Studio had won the design competition[1] for the same project. It was G's first win after coming back from the Land-of-Watches-and-Banks. However, it had died a premature death. The Finance MD[2] had himself called and broken the news.

'We have selected your design, but...'

'But...?'

'We really like your design, though...'

'Though??'

'We want to build your design, however...'

'Thank you, Sir. Please explain what is but, though, however?'

---

1. *Architecture Design Competition, which gives architects the chance to be recognised and win public project commissions.*
2. *Managing Director.*

'Minister M wants us to give the project to another architect. We can't say no to a minister.'

'It's unethical, Sir! This doesn't happen in the Land-of-Watches-and-Banks!'

'You should now land in our country, mentally too! Rush! Now only a call from the Chief Minister's Office can bring the project back to you.'

G was heartbroken. What chief minister, G didn't even know a government peon. In the Land-of-Watches-and-Banks, he had had a chance to stay in the ex-president's house and had even casually tied his turban on the curious ex-Head's head. But this was the Beloved-city-of-A-Bad. The next day, he read in the newspaper, an obituary of his design, the project wrongfully given to the Minister's chosen architect. Now, a couple of years hence, the chosen architect's building was crumbling down. It was as if the ghosts of G's unbuilt designs had taken their sweet revenge.

Poetic justice for G, however, maybe for the ghosts it was not over yet... Decades passed. It was time for another competition, another corporate, another patron; this time it was the Institute of Developers[3].

'Let's take part. We have heard so much about your competition days[+],' A the Architect[++] wanted some action at the M-Ass-Studio.

'Those days we didn't have work.' G was just not keen.

'As if we have now… Developers have maximum number of projects. We don't even attempt.' A the Architect was adamant.

'Who wants to do flashy designs? We will never win.'

+   *Refer to the story, 'Only Time Would Tell,' page 111*
++ *Refer to the story, 'ATS: Anti-Terrorist Squad,' page 59*
3. *Real Estate Developers.*

'They are paying to participate. If we refuse, we will never get any projects from them.' G was warned.

'What do they want?' relented G reluctantly.

'Their corporate headquarters!'

'Corporate headquarters!!? Really?'

Just then, there was a waft in the air. Had the ghosts of the previous project come calling? A the Architect felt her hair.

'Dig those drawings out!' G was possessed. 'See if we can use our previous Finance Headquarter design, it'll save time and expense.'

Drawings of past projects usually lay buried at the bottom of the chest, rarely disturbed by anyone. Once in a while, a crumpled corner of the drawing would peek out of the chest, only to be swiftly shoved inside with no one watching. Pulling out a drawing would mean the mystic ritual of unfurling and unravelling the mysteries of a bygone era. The drawing would be dusted, wiped and smoked clean, while G would stand back and tell telling tales of many a soul who had tread this path before, leaving their indelible mark.

As the drawing was being unrolled, there was a rustle in the chest. Restless, A the Architect felt her hair.

'The brief fits more or less. But they have asked for a building open to the public, and here it is all closed with large blank façades.' A the Architect studied the old drawings and reported her difficulty.

'Make them 'open'able for events, so they disappear from view,' was G's quick fix.

'Three storey high walls that disappear?' A the Architect was curiously serious.

'Only for the proposal! Also, make those walls a bit colourful,' added G.

'Colour? The past ones are all grey.' said A the Architect.

The ghosts of the past design were being exorcised and embodied to the new time, place and clients.

Just then, a passing cloud cast a charcoal grey shadow. A the Architect quivered and felt her hair.

'Developers like flashy buildings, the colour is only there to get us the project.' G reasoned.

'I wouldn't colour.' A the Architect was dead set.

'Of course we won't, dear! If we win, we will convince them to change it back to grey.' G calmed her down.

G was right, the chances were slim. Speculative commercial design was not M-Ass-Studio territory. The odds were completely stacked against us. Winning against their regular architects? In their own game? Judged by their referee? To top it all, if we did falter, our purist peers would be breathing down our necks forever.

It was proposed that the entire three storey façades of the building would either slide, pivot or hinge, making them disappear from view. G's last talisman made all the moving walls red, blue and yellow. It was now on the clients to be open and transparent in their decision-making and choose the design among the competing entries.

And then there was News. The developer community had chosen the 'disappearing' idea over all the other entries. Celebrations started in office. Dead sure that his last talisman was indeed the winning stroke. It was time for G to boast.

'See. My colourful idea clinched it!'

'You want to believe so, so be it!'

The door made a creaking sound. A the Architect sighed and felt her hair.

No one disputed the claim and the project continued. Time went by. People changed in both, the developers' office as well as ours. A the Architect went South. New people who joined kept referring to the old red, blue and yellow façade renders at face value and the intended decolouring was soon forgotten, even by G!

The building was now up. It was time to select the final colour shades - primary or pastel? pre-coated or *in situ*? The discussion went on. No decision was being taken as the façade sheets came only in standard colours and nobody would customise the three chosen colours in small quantities. After a lot of back and forth, the Clients called for a face-to-face meeting to close the matter.

'What exactly do you have in mind? Red, blue, yellow?' asked the Client man, Curiousist.

'Yes, those three. But if sheets come pre-coated, it's the best. An additional layer of paint will fade out soon.' G tried to justify.

'Then our choice is limited. The pre-coated sheets come in none of these three shades,' informed the Client man, Realist.

'You are a strong builder body, why won't they tailor it to suit you?' G kept pressing.

'Why only these colours, may I ask?' asked the Client man, Curiousist.

'Why colour at all?' added the Client man, Fundamentalist, and continued, 'You normally don't use colour in your buildings.'

The air was now getting foggy with suspicion. They seemed to have come prepared.

'You like colourful buildings, no? So, we did it.' G was trying to be considerate.

'For us? Oh, very thoughtful! We never liked those colours from the very beginning. Wondered why You were even proposing them at all.,' the Client man, Fundamentalist took over. 'In fact, we almost thought of going for another architect...'

G sensed that his talisman masterstroke could have cost him the project but kept his *maun*[+].

'...but decided we will convince you to change to your greys later!' Their concerns were an exact reflection of ours.

G was aghast! The ghosts from the past were now showing their true colours.

'Should we keep them just grey then?' concluded the Client man, Realist.

The building happened in grey. Against the backdrop of giant opening walls, the miniscule people seem almost invisible. No matter where you go, the ghosts of your making will haunt you forever.

Far far away in the South, A the Architect gently felt her hair one last time.

+   *Refer to the story, 'You Don't Say NO to the Underworld,' page 1*

Politics of a Lone Tree

'Gushing water! Lovely site!' proclaimed G.

'No trees though? Strange!' I reciprocated, looking at the few odd bushes sprinkled around the new project site near the foothills of the *Ghats*[1]-on-the-West. I made up my mind to plant 1000 trees.

The river was special in a peculiar way. Due to a hydel power plant at the top of the hill, it would get a regular flow of water. In fact, it was so regulated that it operated like a man-made canal, but for its rocky edges and sharp bends that created small waterfalls along the way.

The schedule of the power plant operations dictated whether the river would have water or not; most days there would be a roaring rush, but some days it would be a flat dry bed of rock, and one could literally walk to the barren tribal lands across. It was a surreal play of water that could be switched on or off between the no-more-farming-tribals on one bank and organic-farming-urban-socialites on the other.

The farmhouses of many powerful people dotted this power plant river, and the road was also named the TT Power Road. The adjoining plot we envied for its waterfall presence belonged to a singer-composer from the Hindi movie industry who, we were told, played his flute by the river. We always wondered how he could do his *riyaaz*[2] near that noisy waterfall, where we couldn't even hear each other shout. We always desired the waterfall

---

1. *A stepped terrain.*
2. *Rigorous daily practice to help develop the vocal cords and fine tune the voice in Indian classical music tradition.*

which was adjoining his plot, while he ought to be looking for silence which was in ours. Another typical unfair game of life, we consoled ourselves.

The only saving grace was that due to the slight turn in the river, we could clearly see the waterfall from our site. Hence, the house would be angled near the river edge and freely borrow the view, thus reasoned G. The living-dining space was refined to *Google* coordinates and visually confirmed to be directly oriented to the waterfall. All of us were pumped with the design concept and it was now time for marking on site.

Despite *Google* and visual confirmations, G was still roaming around the site like a water diviner to distil a clear view of the waterfall. After all the acrobatics, he meticulously aligned his body, mind and eyes with the river and declared 'This is it!' The correct height, perfect axis and clear view of the waterfall. It was truly divine, except for a small humble bush in the picture-perfect line of sight.

'Get that bush cleared,' G said in passing to the Man-of-Site and left.

As fate would have it, it was rooted just across the fence in the musician's plot next door. So near, and yet so far! However, as the musician was almost always away, the bush could be cleared at will. Work commenced and the house got anchored in line with the *Falling Waters*[3].

With all the market upheavals, and Clients shuttling between the Country-of-Diamonds and the *Ghats*-on-the-West, the house was shaping up at its own sweet pace. Every time we visited the barren site, while I would push for my vision of planting 1000 trees, G would first peek through and remind the Man-of-Site of clearing that 1 nimble bush.

---

3. *The most famous building designed by one of the modern master architects, Frank Lloyd Wright. It is placed over a waterfall, which is visible to outsiders but, ironically, not from inside the house.*

'No problem, Sir! Will get it done,' assured the Man-of-Site and made a thumbs up gesture.

'Sure? By next visit?' G's mind was fully covered in the bush.

'Yes, Sir! It's just a chop! The branches will flow down the river, no one will even notice.' The Man-of-Site had detailed out the plot.

Months later, it was the next visit. Not even 100 of my 1000 tree saplings were planted, and there was G making a chopping gesture at the Man-of-Site. 'Done?'

'I did go, Sir! Neighbour was playing the flute. Didn't want to disturb.' Man-of-Site made a flute playing gesture at G.

'Do it NOW!' G was not melodious in the least.

'Today is *Amavasya*[4] Sir. We don't touch our tools.'

'No *Amavasya* for me, pass me your axe.' G almost became Parashurama[5] and made a neck-cutting gesture.

'No, Sir! Not today! Please, sure by tomorrow!' Man-of-Site pleaded to save the sanctity of *Amavasya*.

During the long period of construction, the Client had also gotten a whiff of the architect's whim of wanting to shave off the neighbours' unsavoury bush.

During our next site visit, when the house was nearly complete, G took the Client up to the first floor living room. To everyone's shock, it was bush no more, for it had now blossomed into a tree

---

4. *The day of the New Moon holds great significance in Hinduism. It is an auspicious holiday when workers do not work.*
5. *An avatar of God Vishnu. In some versions of the* Mahabharata *he is described as the angry Brahmin, who with his axe, killed a huge number of Kshatriya warriors who were abusing their power.*

thicket that stood out like a sore thumb and hid the view of the Falling Waters entirely.

Rubbing salt to the wound, the neighbouring site had changed hands from the mellow musician to a roaring politician. The musician had left for a peaceful abode; perhaps the thunderous waterfall was more suitable for the politician. A case of one searching for silence, while the other can silence many. We could now feel the power of a tree that hadn't been nipped in the bud.

With my trees now up and standing, I rubbed more salt. 'My 1000 saw the light of the day, your 1 is still not out of its dark *Amavasya?*'

'Today I need the axe more than ever!' replied the rubbed and salted G. But the Man-of-Site had already made a bye-bye gesture long ago and fled, construction had ended with no tools available on site and the Clients had already moved in. With no other options left, frustrated G kept drawing axes[6] in his Red sketchbook[7].

On our next and last visit a few months later, we drove through the grove of 1000 trees, approaching the 1000+1 sore, lone one. The river was gushing and land barren no more. We walked up to the first floor living room. From here, the picture was complete! The living room framed the waterfall perfectly. The Client was happy, but G kept rubbing his eyes with both hands. I rubbed mine as well. The tree had indeed vanished!

'Whodunnit?' we wondered while rubbing in unison.

The Client winked. 'I know the politician!'

---

6. *Also the plural of axis.*
7. *The hardbound and auspicious red* bahi-khata *or ledger books, traditionally meant for preserving accounts over years, are being used by G for everyday doodling since the inception of his practice.*

Indecent Proposal?

G's Friend's wife had already said no.

This Friend was quite sorted in life and had long concluded about wives, 'What is a wife who doesn't say no to everything?'

These were the days when G was young, single and lived happily. The offer was now open to him. 'But can you afford it?' the Friend asked G.

'I don't know.' G sunk his hands into his empty pockets.

This Friend was quite sorted in life and had long concluded about G, 'The moment you have even little money in your account, you travel or blow it off partying!'

His postulates on wives and G, both, were coming true that unusual Sunday morning.

The Friend and his wife wanted an opinion on an apartment they were thinking of buying and had called G to have a look. The wife had rejected it outrightly, even before G arrived on the scene. Those were pre-mobile days and with no way to contact G, the Friend had to wait for his arrival.

'Sorry for calling you here G, there is no point now. My wife has already said no!'

G tried to convince the Friend's wife. 'It is rare to have an apartment open on three sides instead of the usual two. That too, in the centre of the city but surrounded with parks on all three sides. It is also unfinished so you can finish it the way you like.'

'It's also very cheap! The seller is shifting abroad and it is a great opportunity...' added the Friend '...but a wife's No is a No.'

'How would I know?' unmarried G shrugged innocently with hands still in his empty pockets.

'How long will you go on shifting rentals[+]? You need a house too. It's a distress sale. Why don't you buy it?' nudged the Friend.

In the seven years in this Beloved-city-of-A-Bad, G had been made to shift seven rentals. He reckoned that here, since all other occupants were scientists from *ISRO*[1], they would be busy peeping into their telescopes and not into him. Everything fit well, except that it was named Conclave of Eskimos. Name from a -45 degree place given to a +45 degree one? It was still tolerable if rational scientists did not live here. Then he realised that scientists like to give their own names to stars that are light-years away - at least Eskimos are still earthly. This apart, the buying idea, sounded good. He could, once and for all, put an end to his nomadic Eskimo status and settle down in this cool place.

'In case you are interested, you have to deposit the entire amount in a week's time.' The Friend made an I-told-you-so face, taunting G's lac[2]-k of savings.

To give the name its due significance, G thought he could use his frozen assets. Only, he didn't have any left. Let alone frozen, even the liquid ones had evaporated in thin air.

+ *Refer to the story, 'Who Slept in His Bed?' page 63*
1. Indian Space Research Organization, *Ahmedabad. The national space agency.*
2. *Equivalent to 100 thousand.*

The amount was low, but a week's time was way too low too. When G nodded in affirmation, the Friend took G a little away from his wife and asked, 'You have no money. How are you saying yes?'

'I know, but I have a week. No harm in saying yes for now.' G still had not taken his hands out of his empty pockets.

Thanks to the Friend's No-No wife and frantic calls to his clients, associates and PapaG[+], G bought the house a week later. It came with a Single Scientist as his only neighbour.

Still a bare structure of slabs[3], beams[4] and columns[5], it would be another year of construction before both could move into their promised Eskimo land.

'Good to have an architect as a neighbour, for a change. My house needs your input too!' Single Scientist had met G. G wouldn't be able to escape giving free inputs whenever he met the Single Scientist over the process of completing the apartments.

Being a cooperative society, each owner could change the interior walls the way they wanted. G had already started the process of drawing the internal layout of his unit with better alignments and sizes, only to discover that a corner of the Single Scientists' house was jutting into his apartment by 4 feet. 'Why always me!' cursed G. But this is how apartments are built, sold and owned. He would have to live his life with a notch in his Igloo - an irritant in the otherwise through-and-through, wide clean space across the house that he had been dreaming of.

He even sneaked into her apartment site one day and realised that the part sticking into his was disappointingly a functional bedroom and not an ancillary space that he could tamper with,

---

+   *Refer to the story, 'Coronation and Sacrifice,' page 51*
3.   *The horizontal structural plane that forms the floor and ceiling.*
4.   *Linear structural elements placed under the slab to carry loads horizontally.*
5.   *Elements to carry load vertically and transmit them to the foundation.*

even if he ever thought of it. He spent sleepless nights over this protruding notch of the neighbours' bedroom into his life.

Not able to avoid the friendly neighbour's repeated requests, he finally took a redesigned apartment drawing to her. She loved the layout. It was far more open and efficient.

'How much should I pay you for this?' asked the Single Scientist.

'You don't have to pay anything. These designs are all yours.' G began.

'Really? I really like it; I want to make it like this only!'

'What you have not noticed is that by shifting your dining table out of the closed room, you got an extra bedroom.' G was luring her with spatial gifts, 'I also removed the store room from the centre of the house and made your living space bigger!'

'Yeah! The hall looks so much larger,' concurred the Single Scientist, looking at the plans.

'Exactly! So, I pulled the dining table into it.'

'You created a room out of nowhere?' She was keeping a tab on his juggling tricks.

'No no NO NO NO! I have taken your store away.' G was being honest.

'Yes! But I saw that you have tucked the store towards your apartment where the corner bedroom was. It's much better this way.' Opined the far-sighted Single Scientist.

'Of course, the house looks much better and bigger, but the store room is 4 feet smaller than the bedroom it previously was.'

'This is good for me. I don't need a big store area.'

With hands in his empty pockets, G took a deep breath and blurted out, 'Erm…that 4 foot strip has been added to my apartment…,' and continued without stopping, '…I will pay… also get your changes done… at my cost…if you are okay…with my proposal…' G finished it even before he began.

People don't cut strips from their houses to pay as fees to architects, and there was not even an iota of chance that she would say yes. But G went ahead with his indecent proposal. No fireworks, no expletives, not even a fuss. Instead, the Single Scientist politely ushered him out of her house.

First, the name Eskimos; then, isolated on the top most floor with the only neighbour who is single and now these extreme cold vibes that he would have to live with forever. A very bad start to being friendly neighbours.

He came back to the M-Ass-Studio, sad, guilty and jilted, yet satisfied that he at least had had the courage to propose the impossible to her.

Few days later the phone rang. It was the Single Scientist! 'I am okay with your proposal, let's do it!'

Everything went off well. No-No wife said yes to a much larger apartment, Single Scientist got her architect and G got his 8th house + 4 foot strip which he could heartily tamper with.

Work started to merge the critical 4 foot space, and it was only when the shared wall was demolished that G was stupefied. Out came two 18 inch wide ugly columns[+], right in the middle of his through-and-through, clean living space.

Left glaring at these massive unwanted offerings. 'Why always me!' cursed G with hands in his empty pockets.

+ *Refer to the story, 'Additional Reinforcements,' page 41*

Wit •ness to Mat •Haroo (मत• हारो) Spirit

Wet Love

G had fallen in love with his professor. Those were the days when love was not yet corrupted by smokescreens; with real time and space, it was real love too, perhaps! Subtle gestures, hushed tones or even hair blown with the sweep of the wind, swept hearts away. There was love in the air, and G was not spared either. To say that it was platonic would not be entirely true, such a mixed potion of feelings it was that one wouldn't know if it's for the appearance, demeanour or intellect. Whether or not it was reciprocated, relinquished or remained unrequited is difficult to fathom - but unconditional it was and maybe what made it special.

Long before the *Titanic*[1] sank and made live sketching a romantic climax, G would sketch various facets of the Professor, albeit clothed, admiring a myriad of nuances in utter secrecy. The infatuation grew so much that it became infectious. Some male members of the G gang would wait eagerly in the bushes to see the Professor gracefully swing a leg over, kicking and thumping the *Bullet*[2] to life and riding out slowly. Watching this became the most revered passion for them all.

However, like most of G's other passions, it remained largely unfulfilled, until his final semester when he dared to choose the Professor to be his thesis[3] guide. But with G hardly doing any

---

1. *Hollywood movie where the male protagonist draws a nude sketch of the female protagonist, while aboard the* Titanic *that sank in 1912.*
2. Royal Enfield Bullet 350. *Known for its macho association, this street bike from 1932 is the longest running motorcycle in continuous production worldwide.*
3. *A dissertation that presents a student's research and is a prerequisite for a professional degree. Though meant for the semester of six months, students at the School of Architecture commonly, to take years to complete the same.*

work, their encounters became rare. The more time that passed, the more would be the Professor's expectation assumed G, so more work had to be done before the bittersweet rendezvous. This nightmare would continue for days before G could muster enough courage and finally dial from the PCO[4].

'Good morning. It's G, Professor!'

'Morning. G who?'

'I am your student!'

'Oh G! and soo?'

'When can I meet you?'

'Do call me next Wednesday to fix when we can meet.' The witty Professor had all his answers ready.

This avoidance game became the norm as G's thesis was delayed further and further[+]. Weeks and months passed, until one day while riding pillion behind a friend, G was pinched and cautioned of the impending *Bullet* approaching from the opposite direction, just in the nick of time.

With no time to think, react or dodge, G came face-to-face with the Professor, whom he had been avoiding for so long. In a reflex action, G's eyes just closed shut. The Professor later commented in the presence of other students, 'You know…when my students see me…they shut their eyes…like pigeons!' The pigeon and cat affair continued further.

G had started learning how to swim and the friend he went along with disclosed one day that the Professor also swam in

---

+ *Refer to the story, 'Coronation and Sacrifice,' page 51*
4. *Or STD.ISD.PCO: Subscriber Trunk Dialling. International Subscriber Dialling. Public Call Office. From the mid to the late 90s, the yellow public telephone booths with STD.ISD.PCO written in black, were the primary source of telecommunication before the advent of pagers and mobile phones.*

the same crowded municipal pool. It could be G's dream come true, watching the Professor wet or taking a dip; it would finally satisfy all his urges. He would also score brownie points over the other admirers, but it was not so easy. It was like spotting a dolphin in the sea. Months passed and what dol - not even a fin was visible.

Then one day, G finally saw him in the changing room. Their eyes met, but alas! The Professor had already bathed, changed and was on his way out. G cursed his misfortune of only seeing him now: he had missed him by a whisker. His only consolation was that at least the Professor wouldn't know that he had not been spotted free in the waters. Anyway, all encounters would eventually come to a close if G's thesis was completed.

But wait! How can G complete it without me taking you down memory lane to the thesis room in the dark basement? Hold tight.

Located between the thick parallel walls of the School[5], it was a parallel universe. Space here was singular, it had only one dimension - depth! And time? Time didn't travel here. No diurnal cycle of the day and night, no change of seasons. Light was a haze, air smoky, ether abound. A viscous place for primordial questions: Whodunnit? WTF? Whynot? Matters of existence and beyond.

The nocturnal creatures hibernated from one to 15 years of their prime youth here. Yes, you heard that right! That, too, after fagging out five to six years of their customary curriculum. It was long established that the more you were spent, the more intellectual you turned.

One of them slept outside, atop lawned mounds. At dawn, the moment his eyes opened, he would play the flute, the silhouette of him and his instrument complementing that of the mound. Another, with the hypothesis that one cannot conclude a thesis unless one lives through it, had chosen 'death' as the subject of inquiry. He floated between studios in the dead of night, donning dark goggles, gabbing gibberish that would go googly over the heads of his poor peers.

---

5. *G's alma mater.*

The not-so-fortunate lesser mortals paired up for the long and lonely journey ahead. Some enrolled in a photography course and booked dark rooms for that photo finish. Few courageous ones took recourse in the bushes behind the mounds. And the upwardly-mobile ones? They would climb and, of course, pull the service ladder up before plunging deep into the wide gutters on the terrace, with only the stars peeking at them from light-years away.

Wading sluggishly through these hard times, G unceremoniously called it a day in just one and half years. Before we also get trapped in this infinite blackhole of a thesis, it is my duty to pull you back up into the mundane universe we claim as ours.

G succumbed in front of the Professor with three mandatory Xerox[6] copies of his thesis.

'What is this?' the wit master feigned ignorance.

'The document of my understanding on the subject at this very point in time, and Sir, of which you are my guide,' pre-empted G calmly.

The wit master signed the copies without wasting any more time or wit.

Years passed, G's love remained unfulfilled and he was finally getting married. It was to be a day packed with weddings, unfortunately all his own and with the same bride! First was an early morning S religion affair followed by a J religion affair and a third civil registration one, since the couple didn't trust religions. While the families wanted it sealed watertight, he was waiting for the watering hole that Big-Bi's[+] farm would turn into that night, of course of which no photos would be allowed.

Early in the morning, he was on the way to his wedding ceremony

---

+   *Refer to the story, 'Can I Hug You?' page 179*
6. *Pioneers of photocopiers in India. Xerox is the brand name used as a generic term.*

with his few friends and family. As this *baraat*[7] of two cars drove past, it struck G that they had crossed the house of the Professor, with whom he had no contact in all these years. He had to stop.

G walked up the stairs and rang the bell. The Professor opened the door.

'Morning, Sir!'

'Nice *kurta*![8] Where are you off to?'

'It's my wedding, Sir. I want to invite you!'

'Oh! You couldn't resist! When is D-day?'

'Now, Sir. In half an hour!'

'Where in half an hour?'

'Sir, it is very close by.'

'Okay, I'll come, let me put my clothes on!' he obliged.

G was slightly delayed and arrived later than the 7 a.m. time chosen by Head *granthee*[9]. He sat cross-legged[+] with a headache and a consoling Big-Bi on his side, who even got him an *Aspirin*. Through the ceremony, the visibly uncomfortable G kept looking at the entrance door from the corner of his eye. The Professor had indeed arrived, and that's when it struck him!

Earlier that morning, when the Professor had opened the door, he was draped in just a towel. G had not realised that his wish had already come true. Their eyes met again, and this time the

---

+   *Refer to the story, 'Scape Goat and the Cross-Legged Mummy,' page 151*
7. *A celebratory wedding procession for the groom, which usually involves live music and dancing.*
8. *Traditional Indian wear for men.*
9. *Head priest, who also conducts Sikh weddings.*

Professor shut his. Both had acknowledged it in unison, and G stood up for the *pheras*[10].

Later, while blessing the couple, the Professor and the bride Constant K[+] recognised each other. 'Hello Sir, you remember I had come to you to be my thesis guide.'

'Of course, I do! You were the bright one, so I recommended G as a guide for you.'

'Yes! I ended up doing my thesis with him and now see...' said Constant K, smiling.

'Good he didn't pigeon out.' The Professor remained the wit-master he always was.

G was wet with love.

+ *Refer to the story, 'MUAH!!!' page 83*
10. *In a Hindu wedding, this is the ritual where the bride and groom take seven rounds around a sacred fire to be bound in matrimony.*

Only Time Would Tell

Soon after his coronation⁺ at the Hilly-Home-Town and the completion of his thesis¹, G flew to the Land-of-Watches-and-Banks!

While he was away, a not-so-favourite-faculty from his graduation days had been on a design competition² winning spree. Trying to find a foothold in the Beloved-city-of-A-Bad upon his return, G also started taking part in architectural competitions. He rented a 9 x 10 foot corner in a builder's existing office, overlooking the River-by-the-Ashram. In the evenings, when the builder's office closed for the day, it became a place of fun with students, friends and peers drifting in. Especially during hectic competitions, it would transform into a centre for games of Pictionary, forums for laughter and matchmaking pranks.

His team would consist of enthused students, like me, who worked only and only if their strict conditions were complied with.
'If you can wake me up and carry me here, I'll work!'
'Every evening there should be food and drinks!'
'You go sleep in the builder's cabin if you want us to work!'

Money was never a concern, as there wasn't any.

---

1.   *A dissertation that presents a student's research, and is a prerequisite for a professional degree. Though meant for the semester of six months, students at the School of Architecture commonly take up to two years to complete it, and some even took 15.*
2.   *Architecture Design Competition, which gives architects the chance to be recognised and win public project commissions.*

And then a day dawned when all games, forums and pranks abruptly came to a halt. The not-so-favourite-faculty had also enrolled in the same national competition that we were working on. It was the time of reckoning - back out or go head on? Defeat would be too humiliating and a point of no return. Prestige was at its highest stake. The three hand-picked core members, G and two of his friends who were still working on their thesis, the Catcher and the Dreamer - let's call the trio CDG - met secretly. Looking at the sun reflecting in the puddles of the dry River-by-the-Ashram, they took a vow.

'Winning shall not be our goal! If we are beaten by the not-so-favourite-faculty, we shall leave our Beloved-city-of-A-Bad for good.'

In those days, social media was for real and gossip spread faster than the virals of today. Their game plans could not remain a secret. With quite a few double-crossers, both camps were informed about each other on a day-to-day basis. We went into battle, the outcome of which only time would tell.

The preparations were in full swing and every minute counted. The core CDG team met daily at 7 a.m. each morning. The routine was to go out for tea just after they wound up at 10:20 a.m. before the builders' staff entered the office.

G wore - well he didn't wear but carried - a watch in those days. It was the minimal no-markings *Swatch*[3] that he had got from the Land-of-Watches-and-Banks. The plastic wristband, having not withstood the sweat and grime of the Beloved-city-of-A-Bad, had broken off, with no glue nor time to repair. He carried the strapless watch in his trouser pocket and had to just pull it out for just a millisecond to know which quadrant the minute hand was in.

G became the timekeeper, 'Tea time guys, it is 10:23!'

---

3. *A contemporary Swiss watchmaker that was popular with the younger generation at the time, for its economical and modern designs.*

At a narrow 9 feet width, the rented studio allowed only a linear seating layout. While G took his favourite on-the-edge riverside position and the Catcher worked at the far inside end, the Dreamer in the middle had to turn his head either side during discussions.

The Dreamer had surely missed G watch his watch, and one fine day he questioned G, 'How do you guess time so accurately?'

G sensed it instantly: the Dreamer had turned vulnerable. In the nick of time, he held back his expressions and swung along with the good times.

'I watch the birds and the sky!' Catcher caught the wink from G.

The CDG team was now split into two. G and the Catcher who both knew the secret of time, and the Dreamer in the middle who was left looking at the birds and the sky. The prank was on! Overconfident G started telling the time so accurately that his freshly turned and only fan, the Dreamer, started having doubts.

'I'm sure there is a clock tower somewhere across the river!' He scanned the skyline and found nothing.

'Maybe there is a mill siren that you hear?' Over the next few days, he tried but heard nothing.

'Tiffin smell from the *dabbawala*[4] then? But *dabbas* at 10 a.m.? No way!' Of course, his guesses were not holding.

Vulnerable Dreamer was now feeling genuinely challenged. Looking at the bad times he was going through, G and the Catcher consoled him that certain gifts are God-given and not everyone is blessed equally.

---

4. *A person who delivers a* dabba, *or lunchbox, in Hindi. Refers to the impeccable lunch-box delivery system in India, where meals prepared in customers' homes are delivered efficiently to their offices.*

However, the Dreamer stayed determined. 'I'll also practice telling time watching birds and the sky!'

He actually did and over the days, even got very good at it. So much so that it was G's time to feel vulnerable. The Dreamer, of course, couldn't beat the time of the Land-of-Watches-and-Banks, and his suspicion kept mounting. Competition submission was drawing to a close, there wouldn't be such times together. The Dreamer had to catch G red-handed before that. Then one day his time had come. Without checking his pocketed time, G just announced, 'Time for tea!'

As they all stood up, G was facing the inside of the studio, the Catcher facing G and the suspicious Dreamer in the middle. Hit by an intuitive pendulum, Dreamer swiftly turned to G, cornering him without warning, 'Tell time Now!'

G knew his time was up. His hand almost reached his pocket but with Dreamer watching, better sense prevailed. He couldn't afford to lose his one and only fan, come what may. He turned defensive. 'You can't squeeze like this and get time out of me. I need to be in my awakened state!'

'I caught you; I knew all along there was a trick...' Dreamer was ecstatic.

G looked out of the window and continued in desperate defence. 'Can you even see one bird in the sky...?' Adding to G's fatal timing, a bird just flew by.

By this time, the Catcher standing behind the Dreamer had already seen the time on his own watch and signalled to G with his fingers 10 and 7.

'...It could be 10:17' said G in a matter-of-fact tone, putting his hands into his pockets.

'Show time!' Dreamer turned to Catcher. Confident Catcher complied calmly and showed his watch.

Order was restored within a fraction of a second.

Vulnerable Dreamer fan was awestruck. The Catcher was in splits and with no place to hide his face, he went down on his knees, touching G's feet and exclaimed hysterically, 'Swami Awakananda[5]! *Tussi Timeless Ho Ji*![6]'

Till the Catcher could control his silent laughter, he stayed down at the feet of Awakananda: The Timeless one.

When the competition results were announced, the CDG team stood fourth out of the total five positions declared, and the not-so-favourite-faculty's name didn't appear. G didn't have to leave the Beloved-city-of-A-Bad for good and went on to live happily thereafter.

While the Catcher and G were flying high because their prank had stayed a secret, the no more vulnerable Dreamer actually became an accurate foreteller of time, simply by watching the birds and the sky.

---

5. *A parody of Swami Vivekananda, one of the most influential philosophers and social reformers in contemporary India.*
6. *'You are Timeless!' in Punjabi.*

Yearning for Love
🌶 🌶

Propose now or it'll be too late! G had not been able to muster the courage yet.

Even though he had done it a few times successfully, it always feels like the first time. Same dil[1]*-emma, same heartbeats! The time was ripe for the most crucial revelation; a slippery move, like walking on thin ice. I have seen relationships get sour, diluted or dissolved beyond recognition once he bares.*

'Again bare finish[2]? Are you off your head?' T[+] was already waving a red flag.

'You are becoming more difficult than a client!' G countered.

'They are not the concrete types!'

'Highly educated and well-travelled, won't they appreciate the logic and the look?' G tried to construct a convenient profile for the newfound clients.

'Do we always have to change their lives?' T tried showing concern. It was more of a concern for the M-Ass-Studio's survival.

+   *Refer to the story, 'ATS: Anti-Terrorist Squad,' page 59*
1. *Heart in Hindi.*
2. *When concrete walls, slabs, columns and beams in a building are left in their natural deposition and not covered with plaster or cladding. This honest look is however not easily palatable to the public at large.*

'I find the Lady very reasonable; she is our best bet!' With that statement from G, T gave up.

G was dealing with these new clients in the South. They had chosen G to be their architect, contrary to the preference of their friends and family, who suggested going with someone local and popular. The Lady of the house was strong-minded, firm and decisive. The decisions that were taken were thoroughly discussed, debated and analysed for checks and balances before being put into drawings.

For concrete to come in, the timing has to be right. If mentioned too late, it becomes difficult to change the construction method; if mentioned too early, it is the case of a stranger dictating you to live life differently. We were somewhere between that too early and too late stage.

The day had come to lift the veil. A beautiful 3-dimensional view of an all-concrete house was rendered by an intern. G and T had carried it with them on their scheduled visit.

'The foundation will soon be done - can we see what our house will look like? Hope we can get enough sun and green even in this small property of ours.'

The husband was eager to see and get on with it, but the Lady of the house was out and nowhere to be seen. As T started to dig for the render in her laptop bag, G sensed it wasn't the right time and intervened, 'We are still working on it. Will show it to the entire family on our next visit.' T looked inquiringly at G.

She took the matter up with G at the airport on their return. 'You got cold feet, no? Knew concrete will never be accepted.' T's flag was still flying high.

'No! He likes greens and blues; our render is bland and grey. Plus, the Lady wasn't there.' G tried to explain.

'You know she has asked for a full-on white marble *mandir*[3], she would have never approved of your concrete.' T knew white marble and grey concrete are always at loggerheads.

'Close off the *mandir* inside a room. It won't interfere with our space.'

'Very easy to say, there isn't any room left!' T told G to keep his God-trapping ideas to himself.

It was turning out to be a good project. All requirements were meticulously addressed and incorporated. Most were rational, like reduction in passages, efficient layouts and ease of services that we nevertheless enjoy. On their next visit, G and T carried a slightly improved render. Taking a hint from the previous meeting, thriving greens and a deep blue sky were added to offset the bare greyness of concrete.

G told T to start with soft spots.

'Here is your *mandir*! It can open out into the living room for large gatherings.' T showed the plan.

'Very nice! We have religious gatherings quite often; it'll be so convenient.' Approved the husband.

'All your weddings will happen from here only!' said the Lady looking at her three daughters.

'What will you do mumma, when we all are gone?' said the second daughter. The mood was turning sombre, with tears about to form deep in their eyes.

'Bring out the grey of concrete to go with the gloomy air? NEVER!' reckoned G internally.

---

3. *A Hindu prayer space which is usually ornamented.*

'We will get a puppy.' The Lady lightened the atmosphere in front of the visiting architects.

'Mumma! So, the puppy will replace all of us, *haan*[4]?' spoke the third. The scene was still immersed in deep emotion.

'T, please add a dog house somewhere. Now, let's discuss the progress of the contractor's work!' said the visibly moved husband, brushing aside the matrimony matter.

'Sure, I'll add that.' said the always positive T, not realising that concrete matters were getting lost between dogs and Gods.

Back at the airport, T's flag was at full mast. 'Don't try your pinker pig plot[+] here, they'll never buy your grey concrete.'

G came back and asked the intern to tweak the render a bit more for the next eventful visit. It would be the last chance. On the next visit, they finally found the family together and not gloomy with matrimony matters. It seemed like the right time to let the concrete cat out! As T unrolled the render slowly and carefully...

'Is this all in concrete or…'
'Hmm, what's that…?'

While the husband and the daughter were midway through their grey reactions, came the defining voice from the Lady, 'Oh! Sooo beautiful…!'

'Hmm, could we have another…?' the visibly unmoved husband was continuing his call for more options.

'The High Command has approved, let's put this matter aside and now decide where we are placing the pumps and fuses.' G was quick to intervene. It was this immaculate Govinda timing[++],

---

+ *Refer to the story, 'ATS: Anti-Terrorist Squad,' page 59*
++ *Refer to the story, 'Riding the Curve,' page 159*
4. *'…Yes?' in Hindi.*

G had honed over years of rejections. In one shot, he had given the deserved place and respect to the Lady and got the grey concrete approved as well.

The house got built beautifully in concrete and the family lived happily thereafter. The sky and green are captured through various courtyards. Wooden doors enclose the white marble mandir *inside. All pumps and fuses are working fine. T is still holding the flag mast at the M-Ass-Studio. Two daughters have been married and the third is pursuing her studies abroad. An empty dog house at the entrance waits to be occupied.*

In the entire episode, I deliberately forgot to mention a small detail. Let me take you back to the M-Ass-Studio, just a few days before their third critical attempt for concrete approval.

G asked the intern, 'Can you find a fluffy dog with droopy eyes?'

'What, Sir? A fluffy dog?' The intern's eyes turned droopy.

'Don't listen to him!' T rolled hers and whined.

'It should be yearning for love!' G specified further, ignoring T.

After intense research and diligent sorting, an image of a fluffy dog with the perfect droopy eyes was approved by G and faithfully pasted in the all-concrete render by the loyal intern.

The droopy eyed fluffy dog's contribution in the grey concrete approval was soon forgotten, and the render now remains hidden somewhere in the M-Ass chest of drawers⁺.

+   *Refer to the story, 'Ghost Behind the Disappearing Walls,' page 89*

Wit •ness to Mat •Haroo (मत• हारो) Spirit

Monkey Business
🌶

Even lovers loved louvres[1]!

The newly built Government Hospital in a poor and industrial area of the Beloved-city-of-A-Bad was designed with a huge internal garden kept open to public. It had become a popular hangout for people of the non-descript neighbourhood, come patients or lovers. From the OPD[2], the garden was always seen through a line of louvres. They had been meticulously installed after a long and painful process of convincing the clients that the louvres would stop the harsh sun, rain and animal ingress, while keeping the OPD cool at a fraction of the originally intended cost of air-conditioning.

The louvres were looking good and the sun made them hot, creating a natural draft that pulled used air out and kept the interior at a comfortable temperature. G loved his own idea so much that he decided to ape it in his new M-Ass-Studio, currently under construction. But he wouldn't stop at just wrapping the studio in louvres, as there had to be a twist in his tale. Now, he wanted them to be adjustable as well, that too, at half the cost. So, the hunt began for the thinnest steel sheet: stiff enough to span across, light enough to move easily and, of course, easy and light on the pocket too.

However, there was another complication. A few months after the opening of the Hospital, G had found that the louvres were not fool-proof, smart-phones being the culprits. While talking on their phones,

---

1. *A set of directional slats fixed at regular intervals to control the amount of light and air that passes through.*
2. *Out-Patient Department in a hospital*

people would look out to the garden, standing against the louvres and using the lowest one as a footrest. The lower louvres took the brunt - as chats got more animated, more stresses got transferred, twisting and creasing them. After fastidious mental computations and visual interpolations, he concluded that the bending of the louvre was directly proportional to the intensity of the conversation and added this as Newton's fourth law.

Fortunately, this smart problem of phones did not apply to G's upcoming M-Ass-Studio. Personal phones were banned from the time G once spotted everyone engrossed in their own phones rather than in their drawings. On counting a total of 17 live phones in the M-Ass-Studio that day, while there were only 10 of us, he had declared in an instant,

'We will pay your bill, just don't use your phone in the studio!'

Another system was added. It became the G-System Code +9198.

Now, although phones were silenced, there was another primal fear. The new M-Ass-Studio on the outskirts of the city was replete with wildlife, with visiting monitor lizards, *nilgais*[3], giant cobras and even invited elephants. Monitor lizards won't climb louvres, *nilgais* won't jump over the high plinths, cobras won't cross the snake pit and elephants would have to behave when they were invited. But what about our own ancestor? The ever-jumping monkey! What would happen to the louvres? G quickly classified it as dynamic load[4], and simply transferred his load into the lap of PapaG's structural team[+].

'We need the thinnest possible louvres that'll take the load of a monkey jumping on them!'

Used to such rudimentary structural assignments from G, PapaG's team calmly set about to work. After a few days of

---

+   *Refer to the story, 'Loaded Donkey and the Flying Carpet,' page 169*
3. *Blue Bull in Hindi. Largest Asian antelope, endemic to the Indian subcontinent.*
4. *A load that changes over time. This exerts more force than its static equivalents.*

number juggling and mind-bending, they raised their hands. 'We checked the entire Structural Code Book. There is no code[5] for jumping monkeys!'

One way or the other, this age-old problem had to be solved.

'If we can't find one, invent one!' was G's *mantra*[6], and he came up with his own Load Code for monkey impact. A new day would dawn in the history of structures, as samples of louvres were made in different thicknesses of steel to test and devise the newly formed Code.

All was set, but there was a small hiccup. Where would we get a live monkey from? Monkeys are not elephants. They're more like us humans, so they can't be invited and made to behave. Even if we did find one, how to make it to jump precisely on the samples? Who would train?

Train? G pulled out his lateral thinking cap and called out to a trainee from the studio, the lightest of them all.

'We are testing these samples. Feel at home! Be yourself and jump!'

G's hands-on instruction was followed literally; some samples got bent and some did not. The long pending problem of the impacting ancestors was thus laid to rest.

A new generation, primate-proof louvre sample was ready to be applied all over the M-Ass-Studio. No wonder they call internship here a Monkey Business!

---

5. *Standard Code on Structures. The code book that provides the guidelines and standards for the design and analysis of structures.*
6. *Motivating chant in Sanskrit.*

Wit •ness to Mat•Haroo (मत•हारो) Spirit

Unwanted Child
🌶 🌶 🌶

An unwanted child was born and there was nowhere to hide.

Too late to argue whose fault it was and who didn't do enough to prevent it from coming. Anyway, whoever the culprit was, fingers would only point at G. Had it been at a church it was perhaps easy to confess and absolve his sin; after all, to err is human. But 'to err is human' in a hospital?

G told me about an incident at La Tourette monastery and chapel in France, where the contractor had cast a portion of concrete wrongly during construction. The Master architect Le Corbusier, upon his visit to the site, noticed this. Instead of asking to break and recast the concrete, in a gesture of humanity, he simply asked the contractor to inscribe the words 'To err is human' right above the casting mistake. We have never found any reference to this story, and it seems this is probably another case of G's 'Believing is Seeing[+].'

No matter how much he scrubbed, he wouldn't be able to wash his hands of this. Some mistakes are forever. In G's case, with his unusual creative exploits, there is always a high probability of unintended offspring, especially when conceived brutally[1] in concrete. A glaring mistake was staring right in his face. Meant to be hidden within the neat folds of the slim staircase, the beams[2] were, however, cast wrongly, and the outcome was just

---

+   *Refer to the story, 'Believing is Seeing,' page 23*
1. *Brutalist architecture is a style characterised by a massive, monolithic and blocky appearance and rigid geometric style and large-scale use of poured concrete.*
2. *Linear structural elements placed under the slab to carry loads horizontally.*

too unsightly. G was hapless.

G likes to believe that he is a man of systems and gets a Gin-O-Logi[+] high on mixing them frequently. The more systems he erects, the more they collapse. One of these, G-System X/X/O, is the great ritual of crossing out, correcting and highlighting mistakes in drawings using mark-errs. It is a process that has evolved over years, with special colours assigned to each category of errors. I don't know how effective the system is but at least it makes the banal black and white drawings look like a vibrant quilt.

A mistake in a drawing can be crossed out, corrected and highlighted. But what about those etched in concrete? Let's leave the unwanted stair in the custody of hapless G, to let him mull over the problem. We will move to another department of the hospital where everything is upright.

The large Government Hospital[++] building was almost complete and meant to serve the poorest of poor patients. To be frugal, it was built in robust concrete. For some months now, the Clients were pestering G to do some elevation treatment on the plain grey concrete façade, with a desperation that is similar to a family wanting to gift wrap their newborn for the world. They were okay even if the treatment was just at the main entrance. This area was marked with an 80 foot high tower, following G's obsession for all things vertical[+++]. Combined with the horizontal canopy of the porch, the two formed a large cross, an apt landmark for a medical facility. This was, of course, the planned one, well executed and fully legitimate.

A legitimate child meant purely for display?

'Why treat a sound elevation? Why not treat 1000 more patients instead!' G resisted, reminded of the labour pain that the building had endured. It fell on deaf ears. Sick of being patient, he finally gave in.

+   *Refer to the story, 'The Old Monk Who Bought Gin-O-Logi,' page 15*
++   *Refer to the story, 'Monkey Business,' page 123*
+++ *Refer to the story, 'GDP and Sin-Tax,' page 131*

G-System X/X/O of colour coding and highlighting came to his rescue. He used the highlighting *mantra*[3] and got the large cross painted in blood red, as if oozing out of the bare concrete. This solved the problem of the legitimate child, the concrete cast correctly as desired.

However, somebody had yet to own the ill-legitimate love child - the criss-cross beams under the staircase - that we left behind in the other department. Let's go check on the unwanted staircase in the custody of G.

G was hapless. Whether it was guilt, remorse or penance, the beams were like crosses stuck in his throat, which he could neither swallow nor spit out.

'Do you have some red paint leftover from the entrance? The *kaala tika*[4].' For G, the red paint was similar to the black mark applied to a baby's face to ward off evil by making it imperfect.

'Why *kaala*? The red is looking good!' opined the clueless Client, happy with the paint, still wet at the entrance.

'Yes, Sir, we had ordered a drum but used only a third. It was just a cross. Should we paint the entire front wall too?' asked the Contractor, sensing an extra work opportunity.

Cross G wanted to empty the remaining two-third of the drum on the Contractor's head.

'Thank you so much Mr. Contractor, the red cross is good enough. Come, I'll show you something else.' G led the Contactor and Client to the scene of crime - the staircase - and pointed out the wrong beams to them. 'Just paint these bloody beams in red too!'

---

3. *Motivating chant in Sanskrit.*
4. *A Hindu practice of warding off evil spirits or the evil eye by marking a black spot on a person's forehead or on an object.*

'Okay, Sir!' said the Contractor with an indifference, while the Client looked flummoxed.

I still wonder who of the three had fathered this mistake.

The beams were painted red before the dawn of next morning. True to his drawing systems, G had crossed out the mistake in reality, and highlighted it using the leftover paint as a colour mark-err, where he couldn't use an eras-err. Of course, those beams would only get a step-fatherly treatment.

With all the kick of handling this unwanted child, the Contractors actually never got head or toe of the painting solution, and asked very innocently, 'Why only these beams in red, Sir? Why not the entire staircase?'

After a pregnant pause, G delivered in all honesty, 'Can't hide a mistake? Highlight it!'

Epilogue:

Having found a new item to bill, the Contractor kept pushing to paint the entire building red. Somehow, at least this time, G did enough to prevent it from coming.

Today the unintended staircase castings stand red, crossed and highlighted just like his quilt of corrections! Thanks to G-System X/X/O, the unwanted child also feels it belongs.

GDP and Sin-Tax
🌶️ 🌶️

In one severe blow, the entire structure was brought crashing down. The tower had been silenced.

The news reached G. Heartbroken; he too went *maun*[+].

We will come back to this crash in a little while.

Every time G looks at ugly Sintex[1] *tanks crowning rooftops, his mouth waters. He imagines the lost opportunity of sculpting a monumental shape out of it. I have known his standard game for long, of classifying given functions into a kit of parts. A complex brief would be thrashed out and reduced to planes, solids, cylinders and, of course, a tall vertical cuboid in the form of a tower.*

Since his earliest designs, his obsession with the dearest of all his elements has been alive and kicking. It would surely have to be a functional entity, either a lift shaft or an overhead water tank. In other words, the obsession is disguised either as a solution to the difficulty of taking people up or holding water in potential pressure. He must be thanking Newton for having found gravity, which keeps generating these need-based elements to his defence, which are then manifested majestically into a symbol of sorts.

No one at the M-Ass-Studio escapes this ordeal, not even me, who toiled with sweat and blood trying to resolve a spiralling tower for a riverside

---

+   *Refer to the story, 'You Don't Say NO to the Underworld,' page 1*
1.   *The world's largest producer of plastic watertanks, and founded in India.* Sintex *is the brand name used as a generic term.*

resort[+]. That was still a playful resort, but now in his lap was a project for a no-nonsense **Dharamshala**[2]*, that too for the J Religion, to be built on the philosophy of extreme non-violence and austerity. In our madness of keeping everything to a monastic minimum, the building was proposed as simple cuboidal blocks, with a vertical tower that was pivotal in balancing the composition. Not disclosing his own obsessive bias, G feared that this tower without an appropriately assigned function may not hold ground. He tried to subtly convince the unsuspecting clients, the Core Committee of Committed Custodians, C1234.*

'Won't your loaded donors need a lift?' G gave an opportunistic pamper.

'Had it not been for your smart solution with split levels, we would have definitely needed one.' said the Cost Cutter C2/4.

It was indeed G's section[3] that left no scope for the lift. Rooms on both, the ground and first floor, had no continuous connection and were accessed by only a few steps up or down from a mid-level passage. With a lift being redundant and falling down, he now tried to sell the idea of an overhead water tank.

'Imagine what a mess low pressure would cause? Now that all your VVIP's[4] use jet sprays!' G tried the hygienic route this time.

'True. A giant tank is there for the entire campus already. Why duplicate?' The Cautious Calculator C3/4 wasn't easy to budge.

It was impossible to beat business heads in their own game of numbers. Even Newton was failing G. Flustered, he looked up in despair and just then the birds flew to his rescue. He began to chalk out the most critical path immediately, as this would be his final attempt at the *Vertical Limit*[5] to introduce the tower.

+   *Refer to the story, 'Lost Era of the Blu Printagosaurus,' page 75*
2. *Religious guesthouse, mainly for devotees visiting the temples.*
3. *An architectural drawing that portrays a vertical cut through a building.*
4. *Very very important person.*
5. *Hollywood adventure movie, involving a rescue from K2, one of the world's highest mountain peaks in the* Himalayas.

G cast the dice, 'You are taking care of 10,000 cows....'

But he was cut short by the Compulsive Corrector C1/4. 'We have over 12,000 stray cows now!'

G had to manoeuvre through 2,000 more. 'Oh! I stand corrected. You are taking care of 12,000 cows, don't your VVIP donors want to feed a few birds too? And add to some Good Deed Points (GDP[6]) in life.'

'Okay. Let's put a *chabutara*[7] somewhere.' Culture Conservator C4/4 didn't mind the addition of a simple plinth with a pole for the sake of GDP.

'Yes! But not just the plain plinths of the locals, we will make a tall one of the *Nagarsheths*[8].' With that motivational statement, G pinned the tower and silenced C1234/4.

The idea of dishing out GDP in life, had far outnumbered all other recipes. C1234/4 were convinced to spend on, what I would call, a bird dining tower.

G jumped on the opportunity as if he was an aviphile[9], ornithologist[10] and ISRO[11] scientist rolled into one. He dedicated all his time to the research of the nitty-gritty of bird flight, smooth landing, community feeding and en-masse droppings before taking off for new covers[12]. We knew a bit about anthropometrics[13] but never knew we would end up

---

6. *Gross Domestic Product. The monetary measure of goods or services produced within a specific time period in a country.*
7. *Traditional pigeon tower in Gujarati. Constructed for the use of feeding and breeding of pigeons, the structures are a common sight in public spaces.*
8. *The rich and influential trader community in Gujarat, known for settling disputes and preventing invasions by paying off the opposition.*
9. *A lover of birds.*
10. *An expert on birds.*
11. Indian Space Research Organization, *Ahmedabad. The national space agency.*
12. *Unit of measurement in the restaurant industry- a meal or customer served.*
13. *Anthropometrics is the science that defines physical measures of a person's size, form, and associated functional capacities.*

practising avipometrics[14] of sorts. Critical parameters included pivotal distance between the beak and the tail, centre to centre placement for wing flapping, right texture of base for the claw grip and, of course, the means to keep the tower free of droppings after the feeding frenzy that overzealous devotees could cause. It was designed so that the birds would always sit with their beaks in and bottoms out, but never vice versa.

Indeed intriguing. A winding stair contained in a tower full of slots with feeding trays all along. The higher you go to feed, the more GDP you earn. G appended his mathematical analogy to the feeding phenomenon.

Work started on the tower, however a bit late, as the labour had to first finish structures intended for humans. It was still halfway through as the due date for the inauguration came close, and the Cautious Calculator C3/4 took a reductive path. The critically cumulative Core Committee of Committed Custodians found it was faster to demolish the half-done tower, than completing the rest of it before the inauguration day. A violent act, all for a finished look, just for the invited VVIP donors.

In one severe blow, the entire structure was brought crashing down. The tower had been silenced.
The news reached G. Heartbroken; he too went *maun.*

Distraught G could do nothing. The debris was covered with earth and it buried any clue of the tower's humble existence. The tower was reduced to a halo and soon forgotten as the *Dharamshala* was doing well even without one. Days and months passed, and no one noticed the missing tower. Except for the anticipating birds in the sky.

The building remained incomplete in the mind and heart of G. While the donors earned their GDP, G was left wondering which Sin of his he was being made to pay Tax for...

---

14. *A parody on anthropometrics for birds.*

Icci-Puzzi and the Simpleton

'Ummn, Aahm. I see it!' The *shilpcar*[1] moved his palms gently over the model's feline body.

'With your eyes closed?' G was lost as well.

'I just feel her!'

'Should I check if both side curves are same?' G wanted to be a part of it.

'No! No! No! I trust my touch!'

Touchy G waited patiently. The *shilpcar* had moved his fingers over the contours, nooks and crannies and absorbed them internally. He started rubbing the delicate kinks and skirmishes off, carrying on with his final strokes till he was fully satisfied.

'This is my secret life,' G confessed when he took me along one day. 'I steal time out of M-Ass-Studio and come here.'

'Wow! So sensuous!' I myself couldn't resist.

'My Cattivas and my Iccipuzzis!'

It was indeed G's first love[+]. What lay in front of me in this ramshackle workshop was a perfect embodiment of the automobile drawings I had

---

[+]   *Refer to the story, 'Riding the Curve,' page 159*
1.   *Sculptor in Hindi*

made in my early days. I never thought those banal mechanical lines would one day come alive into a shape so sinuous.

But why would he name them Cattiva and Iccipuzzi? Can't they be simple car names? I used to ponder if there were some kinetics behind this or if it was just another one of his mumbo-jumbo mantras[2]. *As destiny would have it, I too couldn't escape the occasion of many naming ceremonies. Those were the days of ink and paper when I would assist in G's automobile concept drawings. I thought these car names came from some complex mechanical engineering understanding, but little did I know.*

As I was finishing my scrupulous drawing, he suddenly charged to my table, 'Let's call it Pauda!'

Car name? I had never even heard the word. 'What language? A Punjabi cuss word?' I prodded him.

'Burmese!'

'Burmese? They don't make cars. They only make mincemeat.'

'...because it was conceived during my visit to Pagan[3].'

'Good, you picked up their language too!'

'Just one word.'

'Wow! A greeting like *Namas-cara*?'[4]

'No! On the way to Pagan, the jam-packed overnight bus stopped in a jungle, and the conductor shouted, 'Pauda! Pauda!'

'Dead of night. Middle of jungle. In militant Burma. You

---

2. *Motivating chant in Sanskrit.*
3. *Ancient city in Myanmar, which is a UNESCO World Heritage Site.*
4. *Name given by G to another creation of his. An Indian sports car whose doors open in a manner similar to a* Namaskara *- a gesture with folded hands used by Indians to greet each other.*

conceived a car?'

'Wait! I thought there were rebels outside and that was the end of the world for me. I was the only clearly outlined foreigner.'

'Spooky! Then?'

'Everyone got out in the pitch darkness and stood on either side of the narrow road, men and women alike, in neat rows facing the forest.'

'Shit!'

'Everyone got out. I couldn't have escaped.'

'A firing squad?'

'Yes, firing it was! They all started relieving themselves in the bushes in unison!'

'Oh goodness! I am relieved too!'

'It was highly disciplined and synchronised; not at all messy!'

'You named your car after a communal pee ritual?'

Why poke my nose into his nostalgia? Pauda *turned out to be a word for peeing in Burmese, but what is the connection? Did he get an idea for the car while doing it? Or was he just marking the creative event and place? Some gypsy tribes name children to mark their travel history or events, and names can be Bridge or Tunnel or even Tsunami. Khasi[5] people name their children after new English words they have learnt from current events, like Skylab Singh, when the* Skylab[6] *was due to fall and Singh was considered brave, or twins from a well-educated couple called Sine Theta and Cos Theta.*

---

5. *An ethnic group from the Meghalaya state in India.*
6. *United States' first Space Station that was launched in 1974. It fell and disintegrated in 1979 due to decay of its orbit.*

'And Zambay?' I was getting jitters but braved looking at the name of another car.

'Let it be, it was a long time ago,' G avoided. Unknowingly, I had meddled in his intimate affairs.

Zambay was a cute looking, small and cosy family car, almost like the *Nano*[7] of today, but from a decade earlier. 'By the same reasoning, Zambay must be some Alpine relieving ritual?' G's dark secrets were tumbling out and I was enjoying his fall.

'Bhutanese! She is not a ritual.'

My arrow had precisely hit his right chamber. 'What? Another touchy one?'

'She was a weaver, my neighbour from internship days[8].'

'And with hardly any work to do, she must have been very fortunate to have you 100% of the time.' I weaved further.

'She had a father! He also didn't work and was always at home. Only went out for archery!'

'Wow! Leaving the two of you alone?'

'No! With my bow in tow, I followed him. Only my arrow reached one tenth of his.'

'Why didn't you break his bow? Even Lord Rama had to[9].' I couldn't stop laughing.

---

7. *Small, economical car produced 'for all people' by Indian automaker* Tata Motors.
8. *It is largely believed that G and three of his friends went to the mountain kingdom of Bhutan as interns and returned after a span of six months. That they earned a lot but did no work, was firmly established.*
9. *In the Ramayana, Lord Rama breaks the divine bow to marry Sita during her* swayamvara, *the Indian practice of a girl selecting her husband from a group of suitors, often based on a skill or power challenge.*

'It's not funny. She weaved a full tapestry for me. Lovely colours, silky smooth. I paid double.'

'True love indeed. Blow your internship stipend on archery and tapestry.'

'Sad, I had to leave the most beautiful period of my life.' G sighed.

'Good you escaped, or you would be living in her cottage with her archer father and her many husbands.'

'Some fallouts of playful and polyandrous society one has to live with!' Thus spoke the nostalgic naive archer G.

Zambay came through some hearty links, decades back, among remote tribes. Car name interwoven with a mountain girl? I was getting dizzy.

A designer's life of producing something is no different from the labour process. After the delivery, one needs to name it too. While naming kids, one can get away with the usual pattern of social trends, but naming projects and products is like going through labour pain again. In naming building projects, G-System Code UNBOND700 came in handy[+]. When it came to cars and bikes, there was no client or site in sight; hence, he was left wandering.

In another instance he uttered Cattiva at my drawing; this time I was prepared and had to corner him.

'So, you now have a real automobile project!' Years of his mental moil were finally paying off.

'It's a blood donation van!'

'One can buy those ready-made white ambulance kinds. Why spend so much?'

+ *Refer to the story, 'MUAH!!!' page 83*

'Make it so seductive that young people flock to give blood voluntarily.'

'Again, those slithering body shapes then?' My provocation was on.

'*Cattiva* means a mean woman, in Italian. Luring her prey!'

'Till his blood is sucked dry…Great!' I had to poke further.

'And he is aware. Yet in three months, he is up and ready to be back with her again.' G was quick to add.

'Even though he has seen others getting sucked dry! Poor thing!'

The name evolving pattern has an interesting human history. Some rely on Gods, mythology characters or even professional practice. A great botanist was obsessed with private body parts while naming plants, resulting in Linaria Vulgaris, Justicia Ovata *and what not. Now it was my mission to get to the root of his other naming scandals.*

However, G's name game was getting on my nerves as there was no clear pattern to slot it into, so I hesitantly dared to ask about the ultimate hyper-car drawing on the board, Iccipuzzi.

'Iccipuzzi? Cattiva's sister-in-law?' I cut the pleasantries.

'There was a simpleton in a wild party, and met a woman who had the hots for him,' he began.

'Hots and then what?' I was in for a juicy story.

'Even after multiple suggestions from her, the simpleton was simply not getting it.' His stress on the simpleton was making me believe more and more that it was G himself. He continued, 'Finally, the woman lost all patience and said it clearly!'

'What?' I kept pushing.

G continued his narration.

'I have got an itc..y pu..y,' she said, looking straight at the simpleton. He replied, 'That's really amazing! But sorry, I'm not into exotic Italian cars!'

Epilogue:

We move to the present day. I was visiting the M-Ass-Studio for my routine work and stay.

'Iccipuzzi has been handpicked by a film director to be Apte's car in their new TV series[10]!' said G, pointing to the cobalt blue exotic standing outside the studio. The car had indeed taken shape. He had just mentioned my recent celebrity crush and Iccipuzzi in the same breath.

'I am bowled over since I saw her long back in Stories by Rabindranath Tagore[11].*'*

'So very Apt-eh?' Both agreed in unison.

---

10. *A science fiction comedy on an OTT platform that includes automobiles designed by the studio.*
11. *A series on an OTT platform.*

Wit •ness to Mat •Haroo (मत• हारो) Spirit

Damsels and Dumb-bells

As the older brother opened the cabin door, the earth moved under his feet. Standing on top of his executive table was feather-light Yogini D, and under her feet, lying belly down and moaning, was his younger brother, Fully biceped A-The Biker!

*

Yogini[1] The Doctress:
It was time for another visit to the starry Megapolis-on-an-Island.

Fully biceped A-The Biker had an unbearable pain in his back. Yogini D had come to see him for G's work, but being generous and a yoga teacher herself, she had offered instant relief by climbing up on him. It was another matter that he would never be able to explain this to his older brother. He was the chosen contractor for G's seaside site outside of the Megapolis-on-an-Island, and she was the coordinator from the M-Ass team. While Fully biceped A-The Biker would consume only powder of protein, Yogini D sustained herself only on solar energy while preaching nutritious diets to the young and the rich.

I would meet them onshore for sure, during our offshore site visits. Well, sometimes not so sure! Sure, only when G could catch the first 6 a.m. flight from the Beloved-city-of-A-Bad without delay - delay not before catching the flight, but after catching the flight. From here on it would be a perfectly oiled routine. Seated in the aircraft such that he is the last one to board the runway

---

1. *A female master practitioner of yoga in Sanskrit.*

bus and the first to jump out, finding an Open slot to Pee without a Queue, Racing cabs, Skipped red-lights, Tedious sprint to the jetty; U*p in the air*[2] actors could learn a thing or two from the fully synchronised and orchestrated G.

Yet more often than not, G only saw the back of the 8.10 a.m. catamaran rather than being on it[+]. Once missed, he would have to wander around aimlessly till he could take the next and slower boat at 9.25 a.m., that too alone. Catching up with Yogini D was a highly grilling steeplechase and the more he timed himself right, the more he would be at the mercy of time. He would do anything just to avoid a glimpse of Yogini D floating away from him, but mostly he couldn't.

*

Fully biceped A-The Biker:
It was time for another visit to the starry Megapolis-on-an-Island.

Fully biceped A-The Biker was the one who took G to the Hindi movie industry.

'We work a lot with them. These actors are mad people. They don't treat their architects and contractors well. The last architect was slapped by the toughie SS.' G had been warned.

'Why take me to them then?' Concussed G asked Fully biceped A-The Biker.

'*Arrey*[3] no no, this one is a family man. He plays mad characters only in movies, plus he likes your work.' And so was fixed the rendezvous.

+   *Refer to the story, 'Moha Maya,' page 193*
2.   *2009 Hollywood movie, where the protagonist is an efficient frequent flyer.*
3.   *Expressing surprise or alarm in Hindi.*

*

Kamini[4] the Seductress:
It was time for another visit to the starry Megapolis-on-an-Island.

'Would you like some lemon in your tea?' Here was the queen of a million hearts, the graceful lady behind colourful chiffons in the most romantic of songs, offering G some freshly squeezed citrus juice.

Two consecutive super hits had made Kamini a superstar. Under the guise of emotional love stories set in exotic locales, both movies showed such a regressive attitude towards women that it left them with a shallow reflection of themselves.

Puzzled at the diva's reel-image versus real-life simplicity, G put aside his Gin-O-Logi[+], and immersed himself in a hearty tea ceremony with Kamini. It left a stain so indelible in his memory that no lemon worth its salt could ever remove it.

G, however, was reminded of another movie where Kamini lodges a police complaint against the wayward advances made by the male protagonist. 'Look at him, Sir, doesn't he look like a rapist?'

Later, that male protagonist of reel-life ended up with Kamini as a real-life husband.

*

Man-with-Dumb-bells:
It was time for another visit to the starry Megapolis-on-an-Island.

While G was busy sipping lemon and tea offered by his wife Kamini, the star was calm and trying out dumb-bells with his coterie of Men-with-Abs. Having started his career as a stuntman,

---

+   *Refer to the story, 'The Old Monk Who Bought Gin-O-Logi,' page 15*
4.   *The daughter of Lord Kama Deva, the god of love. While her parents invoke love and lust in the minds of all people, she induces lust only on the minds of married couples (Source: Naveen Sanagala, hindupad.com)*

he had come a long way and was going steady. The short talk with him was positive and a deal was struck. The M-Ass-Studio would be building a vanity van for the Man-with-Dumb-bells. It would be G's short brush with Hindi movie celebrities and their humane world.

*

Rati[5] the Temptress:
It was time for another visit to the starry Megapolis-on-an-Island.

'I'm feeling lost. Where are you?' It was G's distress call to Rati.

'Just hold on, I'm almost there!' The recent *Big Boss*[6] winner herself was coming.

Kamini's younger sister, the one-movie-wonder had come to pick G up in her car. She was nice, casual and had no airs. It would be her that G would be meeting the most during the project. She had starred in this one bold movie about premarital relationships where a particular episode had become the talk of the town. G wondered if everyone who meets her is reminded of the same.

Cosy car, babbling Rati, G lost in wonderland - the drive was short and over even before it began.

*

Mohini[7] the Enchantress:
Back in the Beloved-city-of-A-Bad, work on the vanity van was in full swing.

Architect Mohini from M-Ass-Studio was the project lead.

---

5. *The Hindu goddess of love, carnal desire, lust, passion and sexual pleasure. (Source: wikipedia.com)*
6. *A popular reality TV show, where contestants are locked in a house for days.*
7. *A Hindu goddess and only female avatar of God Vishnu, who is portrayed as a femme fatale, an enchantress, who maddens lovers, sometimes leading them to their doom. (Source: wikipedia.com)*

Mohini had a charm and it worked to her advantage. Also to her advantage, was that she was the only Venus in an all Mars automobile denting workshop. She had to show up at least once in three days, and that day, the 100 person workshop would come to a standstill.

The workshop was one that specialised in making fire engines. The young owner had already made a pass at her, 'Call me if there is fire.' She had given him a pass.

Once, when Mohini took along a 7 foot tall curious M-Ass-Studio intern from Poland, they happened to spot a 7 foot long cobra curled under the seat of the van. A close call in an enclosed space!

But not for Mohini. While even the heated cobra was given a pass by her sweet shoo, the Indian sojourn for the Polish intern came to an abrupt end that very day. Up close, he had seen both the snake and the charmer!

G was at his perplexed best. An action-packed workshop, a coiled Nagini[8], the 7 foot tall Pole[9] about to be bitten, an owner smitten, all around the unblemished Mohini, the Enchantress!

There are trysts with destiny and encounters with characters that leave a permanent dent. Everyone tries to keep secret memories of them, as nicknames, login passwords and coded gestures, etched deep inside their hearts. G is no exception to these either. How can he ever forget?

Yogini leaving the shores, caffeine with Kamini, a ride with Rati, the pass by Mohini who can woo snakes; G continues to be inspired by women in their many avatars.

---

8. *The female counterpart of Naga- the serpentine class of semi-divine deities found in the Hindu religion.*
9. *An inhabitant of Poland or a person of Polish descent.*

*

Yakshini[10] the Ecstactress:

Sinuous curves were now slithering, back arched to the point of snapping, ligaments stretched to bow tension. With her, G had gone overboard. Wherever she went, crowds went berserk.

With her voluptuous feminine charm, narrow waist, and sinuous pose[+] she would turn everyone green with envy; let me call her Yakshini. There she was, handcrafted by the M-Ass team for the Man-with-Dumb-bells. A personal Vanity Van!

Epilogue:

It was time for another visit to the starry Megapolis-on-an-Island.

A few months later, it turned out to be a fortunate moment. That day, Up in the Air G was ahead of time. At the jetty stood Fully biceped A-The Biker, Yogini D, G and me, all together. G arrived early allowing us time to catch up and not just catch the catamaran!

'How is Yakshini and the Man-with-Dumb-bells?' G asked Fully biceped A-The Biker.

'He doesn't travel with her. He feels uneasy.'

'Uneasy? What's the full-fledged toilet there for?' G justified his well-equipped creation.

'No! People flock when they spot him now because of Yakshini.'

'Oh! So, is he not going around with her?' G felt let down.

'Of course he is. Driver gets her to the location while he comes riding on his motorcycle.'

+   *Refer to the story, 'Icci-Puzzi and the Simpleton,' page 135*
10. *A class of female nature spirits in Hindu, Buddhist and Jain religions. Characteristics of the Yakshi figure include her nudity, smiling face and evident (often exaggerated) secondary sexual characteristics. (Source: wikipedia.com)*

'Motorcycle? I hope just on one[11]!' G winked at Fully biceped A-the Biker!

---

11. 'Man-with-Dumb-bells' debut in Hindi movies was by stunt riding on two motorcycles.

Scape Goat and the Cross-Legged Mummy
🌶️🌶️

A casually drawn freehand curve by G had unexpectedly been accepted as the concept for a beach house by the Client couple N&A, the silent one and the loved one.

Was it because the curve resembles a question mark? I was curious. Maybe N&A did not pay heed and had other pressing priorities[+].

Swirling and twisting the curve in excitement, the M-Ass-Studio team merrily kept drawing and detailing the unique house for six months. With N&A satisfied and Contractor handpicked, it was time for construction to begin on the pristine sands by the Sea-of-Arabia[++].

But of course, how is it possible for things to move ahead smoothly and without hassle in this revered profession of ours? It was just the lull before the storm.

'Can you show plans to this Vastu[1]-Man we know?' asked N-the silent one, who spoke little. The storm had indeed made a silent landfall.

'*VAA...S...TUU?* Really? You want to show Now? We can't change the direction of the sea anyway.' G tried desperately to

---

+   *Refer to the story, 'Moha Maya,' page 193*
++   *Refer to the story, 'Believing is Seeing,' page 23*
1.   *Ancient faith based guidelines for building that govern the shape and location of spaces and furniture, most often at loggerheads with the context and rational placement.*

hide his shock and make the matter light.

'He is also advising our close friends, the A's, who are not doing bad at all.' N-the silent one had just referred to the biggest name in the business.

'Isn't it a bit too late? Designs are final, plans already submitted for building sanction[2] and Contractor paid mobilisation advance.' G knew he was fighting an already lost battle.

'We are still waiting for the sanction; his *Vastu* inputs can do only good for us.' N-the silent one wanted to be the next A of the country.

How could G explain that elevated pools, basement suites and questionable curved shapes are all blasphemy in Vastu*. Come what may, there was no way a slithering curve lying carelessly on a beach would fit inside 'nine squares with a hole in the centre'[3]- a Vastu-Man's fantasy. Period.*

G wanted to warn N-the silent one, but how could he? Vastu-Man was showing him the heights he had taken the A's to. There was no way to avoid it and the day came for inevitable sacrifice.

'I am Vastu-Man. N-*bhai*[4] told me that he chose you to draw his home. I work with many architects but haven't heard of you.' The look in his eyes was the same as a goat sees in the eyes of its slayer.

'It is very kind of N-*bhai*, we do small buildings.' This small a goat may be pardoned, so hoped G.

'How cute. Costing how much roughly?' Vastu-Man wanted to know which knife he should sharpen.

---

2. *Submission to the authorities for statutory building permission.*
3. *A typical layout of a square building is divided into a grid of nine squares, where the centre called the* Brahmasthanam *is to be kept unbuilt and open to the sky.*
4. *Brother in Hindi.*

'We are constructing about 5 crores[5] worth in our Beloved-city-of-A-Bad, some 2 crores in my Hilly-Home-Town and the rest would be about 10 crores in total.' G said sheepishly. Goats can't gloat.

'That's so lovely! I just got 7 crores worth demolished in J Nagar today. I told another client to immediately dispose their plot of 15 crores. N-*bhai*'s friends just moved out of their 100 crore house because I told them it would never give them sound sleep.' Vastu-Man's mass destructions far exceeded G's humble creations.

'Very impressive portfolio! We have been working on the beach house design for six months now. It's already gone for building sanction too; I can only request that you be reasonable,' pleaded G, as he laid the drawings on Vastu-Man's altar and prepared himself for the impending slaughter.

'I am, myself, a qualified engineer and understand fully well architects' computer drawings. Rest assured, I will ask for the bare minimum changes,' said Vastu-Man, softly flipping through the drawings as if petting the goat.

Engineers anyhow don't like architects. How could G trust a disqualified engineer in the embodiment of Vastu-Man, reborn only to settle scores with architects? It was only a matter of seconds now. The project inspired by a ship marooned on the beach was doomed even before it could set sail.

He had flipped through the drawings. Easy meat, he must have thought.

'I will send you my observations by email after careful study.'

G realised his sentence would now be served in writing. In one glance, Vastu-Man would have seen through it.

'Why not now itself?' thought G. He wanted to get over with the onslaught.

---

5. *Equivalent to 10 million.*

'It is not my choice. Please don't get me wrong! If I see drawings that'll cause marital infidelity or upset stomachs or financial losses, it is my duty to alert my earnest clients,' said Vastu-Man, reading G's thoughts.

It is always the architect's designs that are made scapegoat to the imaginary problems of Vastu.

Vastu-Man continued, 'I can still convince N-*bhai* and A-*ben*[6], but how do I face Mummy-*ji*[7]?'

Mum…mee…jee? Who is this Mummy-*ji* now? Some God woman? A Vastu-*ma*[8]? He did not know. N&A had never mentioned any Mummy-*ji* before. Mum G was now numb G, while Vastu-Man kept reading G's thoughts loud and clear…

'Oh! You haven't met Mummy-*ji* yet? She is N-*bhai*'s mother. You know she lives in a beautiful chateau…in the Country-of-Diamonds?'

Vastu in a chateau from ancient times? The thought crossed G's mind and he suddenly had this pressing last wish to mummify Vastu-Man cross-legged[+], deep inside some cha-tomb.

Back in the Beloved-city-of-A-Bad, waiting had the silence of the lambs. A few days later, it arrived! The killer mail from Vastu-Man.

'Just these four points? Nothing about the questionable curve, elevated pool, beds in the basement?' G was pleasantly surprised to see Vastu-Man's observations kept on his table.

'Yes G, he is only asking for minor changes in some room locations only,' said a grinning Architect H, who had meticulously drawn

---

+   *Refer to the story, 'The Old Monk Who Bought Gin-O-Logi,' page 15*
6.   *Sister in Gujarati.*
7.   *Ji is a suffix used at the end of the name as a sign of respect.*
8.   *Mother in Hindi. Women who are spiritual leaders or considered godly are often suffixed with* ma, *as a sign of respect.*

those complex curvaceous drawings meant for execution.

'Then make those minor changes and send them back.' G wondered why the Vastu-Man was letting the cute goat escape.

Let me tell you how architects tackle mild Vastu irritants in general. By the law of averages, some Vastu points are already in the design by default. Then, by sorting out minor underground services, some more are easily gained and added. By juggling a bit, one or two more fall into place. This dish, then sprinkled with septic tanks and water closet positions, is served to the demanding Vastu-Man, who is more than willing to let go of the few leftover ones.

'His points are completely opposite to our layout. Not even one is possible to change.' Architect H returned to G in a minute. His grin had now vanished.

This was no ordinary situation. Vastu-Man mentioned four wrong locations of activities that were positioned completely opposite to where they should have been. How could Vastu be so anti-G? They couldn't be resolved even if G was born again.

It was not *jhatka*[9], Vastu-Man had chosen slow *halaal*[10] for his goat. What had seemed like soft pleasurable pain were four holes that would slowly bleed the goat to death. The end was close. Star-crossed G escaped to his siesta and came back fresh.

It dawned upon G that the sun had risen from the West today, and the very next day G wrote to N-the silent one: 'What Vastu-Man has asked for is impossible to incorporate without changing the entire design. While we try our best, would you please get him to confirm that there will be no further 'observations' from him?'

---

9. *Killing of an animal in a single strike, with the underlying intention of causing it minimal suffering.*
10. *A way of killing an animal where an incision should be made in the throat, cutting four of the major vessels. Blood must be allowed to drain and the spine not cut until the animal is dead.*

N-the silent one, was prompt. Pat came a mail from the Vastu-Man. 'I am very sympathetic to architects; please rest assured that there will not be any further observations. Just satisfy these four small ones.'

Not only was Vastu-Man confident, precise and surgical, he was also sadistic: sure that the four punctured veins were more than sufficient, he was enjoying the architect killing his own design. Soon the revised drawings were mailed to Vastu-Man. A few days passed without any movement. There was dead silence from his side. And then there was an email...

We will come back to the contents of this email soon. On my next visit to the M-Ass-Studio, I knew well that there would be no curves left slithering. No question of a question mark; all would have been straightened and boxed into nine squares. I did not know how to come face-to-face with the slain G.

'So? Curves squared up? Mummy set inside[11]?' My sarcasm was at its mildest. Mum G pulled out the printed email from Vastu-Man.

'Dear G,

I have not come across a response like this from any architect before. You got all my points covered perfectly without changing a single line in your drawing. Your design is now completely as per my *Vastu*. Please go ahead.

Yours,
Vastu-Man'

How did the goat escape? I ruminated.

'When it appeared that the sun had indeed risen from the West, I

---

11. *Set inside an enclosed ground area or* mandala *of nine squares, which defines the placement of spaces as per* Vastu, *is the spiritual lord or* Vastu Purusha. *He lies with his face down, hands and legs folded, and navel at the centre of the grid.*

just flipped the drawing…' G said with a controlled blush.

'…And all four points fell in their *Vastu* slots!' I made a thumbs-up gesture.

'But wait! Please take note.' G paused and continued with clarity, 'First I took in writing from him - no further observations!'

Mirroring the drawing had worked once again[+].

'So you eventually mummified him cross-legged in his own 9 squares!' I had to add.

The house got built without a single line changed in the design. Marital infidelity or not, the couple had three children together and lived happily thereafter without upset stomachs. And prosperity? It saw no limits and grew by leaps and bounds until the house met its eventual fate[++].

Epilogue:

12 years passed by. No one heard of Vastu-Man again.

While we were editing this story, Client C[+++] called, 'Can you email the plans. We need to show them to Vastu-Man.'

'VAA…S…TUU? Really? You want to show now? We can't change the direction of the river anyway.' G tried desperately, once again.

'Don't worry. Remember, he didn't make you change a single line. He is the same sympathetic one.'

Cross-legged or otherwise, Vastu-Man cannot be mummified, concluded G.

+   *Refer to the story, 'Lost Era of the Blu Printagosaurus,' page 75*
++   *Refer to the story, 'Moha Maya,' page 193*
+++   *Refer to the story, 'Love for Wives and Guns,' page 67*

Wit •ness to Mat •Haroo (मत• हारो) Spirit

Riding the Curve
🌶 🌶 🌶

As always, she was waiting anxiously at the gate. G was rushing, as would happen during all the frequent visits he made to the Coastal-town-of-Kane[1] in those days. For a moment, let's leave the lady anxious and G rushing, and go watch a Govinda[2] movie.

Govinda, in many of his comedy-of-errors movies, is two-timing his love interests and mixes up roles only to juggle out of it in the nick of time. His immaculate timing, balancing acts and knack for negotiating is what gives G a high. The best part is that his love triangles don't have tragic endings. G could never comprehend how two protagonists could live happily ever after if the third had to die or exit the scene, as is the norm. Perhaps, therefore, Govinda movies are G's favourite. I remember watching quite a few with him.

Other than the letter G, there is something else that they both share. It is the art of two-timing their love interests. Unfortunately for G, his two love interests start at A and end at B. It is Automobiles and Buildings, one kinetic and the other static, each of which he manages quite well without severely offending the other. Just like Govinda, he too mixes up roles only to come up with a new and improved A or B. In fact, the solution to a new B may be an offering from A. How ideal!!

G had been awarded a design-and-build project of a prototype petrol pump. Being a petrolhead himself, a high couldn't get higher. Not just one pump, his design to be replicated in

---

1. *Lady fish, a staple in the Southern coast of India.*
2. *Popular Hindi movie star known for his comic timing and dance.*

thousands, that too, by the biggest *Navratna*[3] company of the country. Petrol is not free, of course. After selecting G through the design competition[4], the *Navratna* Chairman himself couldn't believe that such an outrageous design could actually be built.

'Of course, Sir. It may look futuristic but everything is buildable today.'

'Build one and show!' the chain-smoking Chairman threw a challenge.

'We don't build, Sir, we only design.' G didn't want his hands dirty as usual[+].

'I will give you all the money you need! No bureaucracy in between. You have 60 days!' provoked the Chairman between puffs.

'Sir...But...'

'Give me the pump or we go ahead with another designer.'

'But....Sir...'

'We will inaugurate the pump 60 days from today. Either it is both - you and the pump, or none!' The Chairman had given the ultimatum.

Turnkey projects[5] were not G's cup of tea, but he had no choice. He shuttled between the Beloved-city-of-A-Bad and Coastal-town-of-*Kane* every week, making him a proud Jetways Platinum member with extra benefits. The next 60 days would turn out to

---

+   *Refer to the story, 'Coronation and Sacrifice,' page 51*
3. *A group of few companies in the Central Public Sector Enterprises that have enhanced financial autonomy.*
4. *Architecture Design Competition, which gives architects the chance to be recognised and win public project commissions.*
5. *Contract under which a firm agrees to fully design, construct and equip a facility, and turn the project over to the purchaser when it is ready for operation.*

be the most hectic period in the lives of everyone around G.

Putting up this project was even beyond the comfort of his own Gin-O-Logi⁺ zone, and was the mother of all logi(sti)cal sequences turned upside down, as no one seemed to have any clue as to what was happening. The stainless steel structure was arriving from the Capital-in-the-North, the tensile fabric roof from the Ghats⁶-on-the-West, the fuel equipment from the Megapolis-on-an-Island, and the electrical and plumbing from his Beloved-city-of-A-Bad. Everything else had to be found and fabricated locally in the Coastal-town-of-Kane. New place, new role, inexecutable designs and impossible deadlines.

G chalked out a plan, delegated work to his architects, shifted them to the Coastal-town-of-Kane and got them motorcycles to run errands on. Beyond this, he was of no use. His further scope was only to be their agony aunt with a war cry - 'Do whatever, finish it in 59 days!'

Late in the evenings, the exhausted team would somehow drag themselves to the tavern nearby and drown themselves in litres of Vodka and *Kane* curry. Next day, it would be the same tireless cycle.

Among the plethora of problems, we discovered that we would never achieve all the flexible shapes and slaloms required for the curvaceous driveways that G had fantasized about from his F1 addiction. Smooth riders call it 'riding the curve.' Forget execution, drawing his fancy curves itself is not an easy task. After many years of frustration, he had long concluded that computers are no match for the ones drawn by hand, that were inspired by soft feline figures. Software demands too many parameters and lacks tactility and intuition.

During the pre-computer days at the studio, while drawing some of his F1 inflicted sinuous designs, I often had to go through this ordeal as well. He would pull out any thin linear object from the stationery junk, like a steel edge or an acrylic strip - something that is flexible but has the

---

+   *Refer to the story, 'The Old Monk Who Bought Gin-O-Logi,' page 15*
6. *A stepped terrain.*

tension of a bow. He would then place it on edge over a sheet of paper and ask us to hold it vertically across three random points; two hands and one knee or a toe maybe.

'Hold it still! Don't move.'

I am as tense as the strip, then he comes charged, loosening himself, adjusting his body to the drawing board height and in one swift move of the pen like a samurai swordsman, the curve is planted. He then stands back and celebrates how he has captured the limit of that material in tension, and I would say, my tension as well!

When it comes to his love A, there is no compromise and he can go to any extent to achieve the desired curves. Bent steel edges, broken wooden beadings and snapped acrylic strips at the M-Ass-Studio are innocent victims of this bizarre ritual. Thankfully for me those days are gone, I am not the victim anymore, just a witness. Let's ride the curve back to the present time.

On the drawing of this petrol pump, vehicular paths looked like amoeba islands, always a complete loop, however curvaceous. It was day 15 - time to find the kerbs[7] for the curves. With the drawings in hand, G and his local assistant rode to the only casting yard in the Coastal-town-of-*Kane* that could supply precast concrete kerbs.

Looking at all sorts of amoeba shapes in the drawing, the vendor, who knew his kerbs well, said in one go, 'You will not find these curvy kerbs in the entire world, and this is just the Coastal-town-of-*Kane*, Sir!'

While G was engaged with the vendor, the disinterested assistant thought of oiling his rusted motorcycle chain with the discarded oil used for demoulding[8]. In a chain reaction, oil was being re-recycled.

---

7. *The raised edge of a pavement which separates it from the road.*
8. *Removal of the hollow container within which wet concrete has been allowed to set until it hardens.*

From the corner of his eye, G saw the loose chain shaped like amoeba. The disinterested guilty assistant had unknowingly become a sperm donor in the germination. An idea was born.

'The motorcycle chain will become our kerb!' declared G.

'What, Sir? A chain? We don't make auto parts here!' The vendor was puzzled.

G had found all the requisites - identical interlocking units, adjustable curves and fast assembly - in the shape of the motorcycle chain link. Moreover, it was an offering from his first love A, he couldn't have gone wrong.

'Can you make this simple link 50 times larger and 10,000 in number?' G was dangling the carrot.

'Yes, Sir. I can do 10,000 pieces.' The vendor was happy without understanding what had hit him.

After doing multiple sidekick roles as macho bracelets, nunchakus[9], and even a weapon in street fights, never in its dreams had the bike chain thought of becoming a roadside kerb. The order was placed and on day 45, they were delivered on site.

Just like the curve planting ritual on the drawing board, G would get labourers to hold a thick PVC pipe in tension while the assistant would draw giant curves on the ground. As we watched from a distance, the assembled 'bike chain' kerb was sheer beauty in frozen motion.

Just as I had suspected, for the sake of love B, G had of course gone to the other love A, and found solace in auto parts. It was day 58. All curves were executed as drawn; the noise and dust had settled. The chairman landed in his smoky helicopter. The pump opened with pomp and show on day 60.

---

9. *Japanese martial arts weapon consisting of two sticks joined together by a chain.*

It was day 61. Let's go back to the lady. As always, she was anxiously waiting at the gate.

G was rushing. Should he stop at the tavern on the way, for the sake of his teammates? He would be back to his is Beloved-dry-city-of-A-Bad soon. He was faced with this heart throbbing *dil*[10]-emma on every visit he undertook in those days. He could not resist the temptation.

'Hurry, Mr. M!' G was M for her.

'Sorry, I got late.' G had a hangdog look. Perhaps something to do with stopping at the tavern.

'Let's rush, there isn't any time left!' She pulled G's bag from his hand. Once plonked, he would regain his breath and have one last look at her. She would be looking up at him from the tarmac.

'The crew is so nice and care so much for their Platinum members!' thought G, one last time.

As the wheels lifted off the tarmac, G wondered how close he was to being Govinda, before dozing off.

Epilogue:

The 5 crore project was completed in a record 58 days. From Vodka and Kane, the team was back to chai[11] and khari[12] in the Beloved-dry-city-of-A-Bad. Within a few months, the Chairman passed away due to cancer. Jetways, too, wound up after a few years; they don't make Platinum members anymore.

In the known life of G, day 61 was the last time he saw the Jet lady.

---

10. *Heart in Hindi.*
11. *Tea in Hindi*
12. *A thin, flaky biscuit that is a common accompaniment with tea.*

A Piece of Blue Putridity

The pressure was mounting. G had vowed that his inaugural dump would be in royal blue only.

His apartment was ready to move into. The chosen blue tiles for his own toilet were installed precisely, with no residues at the corners. The only component missing was the commode in a matching royal blue.

An element of putrid blue[1]? As far as commodes are concerned, white ones are universal, reasonably priced and would sit perfectly in contrast with the blue tiles.

G was adamant. He had seen a blue one in a brochure, from a company based in the City-of-Round-Rocks-and-Pearls, but it wasn't currently in production. They would produce it if the order was for a minimum of 100 pieces. Either 100 wannabes decide to order at the same time or G makes the entire society of Eskimos[+] sit on royal blue too. It became a game of patience and perseverance, with G standing in a long queue, waiting desperately for his turn.

He was a firm believer that, from the commode, one should always look out into a clear open space in the front and not into a dead wall. It probably came from primordial instincts of relieving oneself in the lap of Mother Nature. Such supreme

---

+   *Refer to the story, 'Indecent Proposal?' page 99*
1. *Phrase for 'filthy rich.' The colour blue has long been associated with royalty.*

levels of luxury in a small sized toilet? No chance. But this desire could be set off easily: by placing the door in front and doing the job with it kept wide open. So, he decided to place the commode right in front of the thick wooden toilet door. *This obsession is also carried over in the toilets of his new M-Ass-Studio, for God knows what reason.* For the moment, the door just opened into an empty drain hole waiting for the commode to arrive.

And arrive it did! It was mesmerising in royal blue. G had controlled himself enough and eagerly got it fitted. Alas! The joy was short-lived. The vile blue thing jutted out a bit extra and wouldn't allow the door to swing open fully. He could never do his business on royal blue and meditate on the same hue. With the long-awaited commode firmly in place, door perfectly installed and tiles already fixed, it was check and mate. Nothing could be moved.

A few days later, G moved into the house and invited us all for the housewarming. It was few close friends and the small team from the M-Ass-Studio. We were all sympathetic to his cause, expecting him to be upset, knowing deep inside that he was not having very pleasant mornings. Changing homes, making indecent proposals and living with Eskimos - what a dyschezic start to a journey that would last at least a decade, if not a lifetime.

To our utter surprise, it was *Deep Purple* playing loud and not the *Moody Blues*. G was at his best and led us to the toilet door. It swung open fully. Magic? Or just an illusion? Did he shrink the door? Or deflate the royal blue commode?

None of it! He was simply nipping the problem where it hurt the most. The small portion of the door fouling with the commode had been cut out so it glided around the curves smoothly and swung open freely. He had indeed had his dream dump with an empty void in front and royal-blue under.

'And the hole left behind in the door?' asked the budding critic.

'Shut and see.' G was waiting for this and pointed to the cut piece stuck firmly to the door frame. As one closed the door shut, the wood grains flowed across, hues matched and they slipped into place, like the final piece of a jigsaw puzzle, and became almost invisible.

This fateful detail became the talk of the Beloved-city-of-A-Bad. So much so, that a student at the School[2] used the same detail without any need in her design, where G was attending as a juror[3]. She was grilled severely by the other members of the jury, 'How could you do something so blatant? Do you want to clear the semester or not?'

The student kept quiet. There was a concentrated pause. She took a deep breath while G held his, and then it came, 'Sir, I saw this detail in G Sir's house.'

The jury members looked at the tenesmus G, who wouldn't be able to preach what he practised.

Epilogue:

It has been 25 years; G stays in the same apartment. He got married[+] and had children. In the renovation a decade after he moved in, royal blue was replaced by a more compact white. The piece of the puzzle remained, but the w-hole thing had become redundant.

+   *Refer to the story, 'Wet Love,' page 105*
2.   *G's alma mater.*
3.   *A panel of architectural experts and academicians that students in schools of architecture present their work to. The jury is in place of a formal examination.*

Loaded Donkey and the Flying Carpet
🌶 🌶 🌶

'I think it's haunted. Three months it's been up there like this. I am really scared,' murmured one donkey loader to another.

'True! I too have been hearing creaking sounds in the night,' seconded the second in a hushed tone.

'Do you know it is standing just on these thin bamboos?'

'Only on bamboo? You drunk? Swear on your donkey!'

'I swear! Never seen such a floating floor!'

'Oh! I will never pass under that. And with my wayward donkey, never ever!'

Not just the donkey loaders, the can-do-anything-contractors and the ever-do-good-friends and there-for-anything-peers, were also overheard. Rumours abound that the slab[1] had been cast mid-air, without columns[2] and was held up on just thin bamboo scaffolding[3].

This floating slab became the object of consumption from a bizarre phenomenon to a subject of ridicule. I also felt it was absurd, G was going a bit too far for everyone's comfort, even taking Newton's gravity lightly. At least he should have spared

---

1. *The horizontal structural plane that forms the floor and ceiling.*
2. *Elements to carry load vertically, and transmit them to the foundation.*
3. *A temporary structure normally made of bamboo and tied together with jute ropes, used to support a work crew and materials in the construction of buildings.*

his ever-pragmatic father, PapaG[+]! Anyway, blame it on the Beloved-city-of-A-Bad: dry, flat land with no boundaries, gossip was spreading free and wild.

'G has cast the slab, now he is looking for ways to support it!'

Dreams coming true can also turn into nightmares. Let me take you under the cover of this floating slab. The 40 x 40 foot slab was conceived about nine months back. The client approached G for a weekend house that would be completely open to nature, yet provide all creature comforts like protection from the blistering heat, blinding glare, lashing rains and infecting insects. The nostalgic mosquito net, which G used to sleep under in his childhood, crept into his mind. He imagined a fully transparent house with no walls, draped just in a mosquito net.

Normally, clients like to shoot down architects' first proposals and end up choosing from subsequent diluted options. So, G makes the first one as wild as possible. The Architect N, who accompanied G on that fateful day, had opened her beautifully rendered watercolour in front of the Clients.

'Here it is. The slab floats over you - no walls, no columns, just a pocket of space netted in nature!' G introduced the impossible idea. It was meant to be like the first serve in tennis, which he could fault on.

'Wow! This is exactly what I had in mind!' The Client smashed G's ace at half-volley itself.

'But... o-k... also...' G's sluggish return was now stuck perfectly in the net, with no escape in sight. He had chewed on his own toe a bit too deep. His team was now left with the daunting task of actually making it happen and keeping the game with the Clients going 'Love all'.

The game was now of doubles and volleys got transferred to the practical structural engineer PapaG. 'It's all trees and

---

bushes, where are the supports?' he asked, looking at the freshly approved transparent pavilion-like structure seen in the watercolour render.

'They are very, very fine and hidden within thin window mullions[4] and in delicate frames for the net!' G was getting poetic.

'No support below, nor above? Only yogis levitate, not concrete.' PapaG only believed in proper supports.

'The slab is held with a deep spaceframe[5] on the terrace. Please look carefully,' G pointed to the thin criss-crosses in the watercolour render, poetic no more.

'This I saw, but I don't want to hang a heavy concrete slab from it and make it expensive.' PapaG was always grounded.

'Then don't hang the slab, make it a part of the structure too,' G kept offering acrobatic solutions.

'You mean a steel-concrete composite? You will have difficulty coordinating the two different sets of agencies on site.'

'That's my problem. Leave it to me!' boasted G.

'How? Unless both steel and concrete are tightly locked together into one, the slab will crash land.' PapaG reiterated the difficulty, but confident G had made up his mind.

For his crazy ideas, he can push all his consultants to the edge. Here, it was his structural engineer and father himself. So, PapaG went about coolly addressing one more tantrum of his overgrown child.

PapaG's solution had all the technical calculations correct, except he did not state the sequence of the concrete and steel parts. Let me further

---

4. *A vertical metal bar between the panes of glass in a window.*
5. *A rigid, lightweight, truss-like structure constructed from interlocking struts in a 3-dimensional geometric pattern that is capable of carrying large loads.*

elaborate on the cascade of incidents that followed.

G was now faced with the chicken-and-egg paradox. If the steel part was installed first, it was impossible to keep it hanging in place while the concrete was being cast. And if the concrete came first, it would have to be in mid-air without any steel supports. Applying his trademark Gin-O-Logi[+] of reversing the sequence, he chose the latter.

'Let the concrete agency start first. Before they remove the scaffolding in 21 days[6], the steel agency will bolt the structure on top of it. It will then work as one entity.'

For the Contractor, it was unsettling. He had only built buildings starting from the foundation upwards. He was now being asked to start from the top, down to the foundation.

90 tonnes of concrete was poured. No foundation and no columns, only bamboo underneath.

And the steel which was to arrive on the third day? At the last minute, the steel agency announced a delay of three months!

Let's go back to the scene of the creaking bamboos with whispering donkey loaders, excuse-making contractors and gossiping do-gooders.

All who were not awestruck were now actually stuck - the labourers, material, contractor's bills and especially G. He had himself created the problem and had kept everything and everybody in suspended animation for months.

Finally, the steel did arrive and was instantly bolted onto the floating slab. It was time to remove the scaffolding.

'You mean remove?' the Contractor had gotten comfortable with the bamboo.

+   *Refer to the story, 'The Old Monk Who Bought Gin-O-Logi,' page 15*
6.   *The curing period for concrete, when it is able to gain 94% of its strength.*

'How else will my client sleep inside Mr. Contractor?' G, already furious with the delay, tried to make him remember.

'It's without proper supports, Sir! How can I risk the lives of my labourers?' In the Contractor's eye, the just installed thin steel columns were not considered a viable support at all.

'Remember you yourself bolted the steel columns?' G tried to shake him again.

'But Sir, there is nothing under.'

'You are a technical person Mr. Contractor! Okay! I'll stand under it, start removing the bamboo.' Furious G thought of other uses for the bamboo but kept his calm.

'And I'll sleep under your slab!' added the Client, who was eager to get what he had only seen in watercolours until then.

As the shuttering was slowly removed, the thin, almost invisible columns made the thick slab float like a flying carpet.

Epilogue:

G called PapaG from the latticed terrace. 'The slab shakes a bit. I can feel it under my feet.'

'It will stop shaking. Just get all other things done.'

'It's all done, only a layer of waterproofing is left.'

'Ever seen a donkey's legs tremble with load?'

'It is 90 tonnes, not donkey load.' The discussion was getting wonky-donkey.

'When you load them a bit extra, they stop trembling.'

After the waterproofing work was done, the slab indeed became stiff. Everything was hunky dory. The house won an international award. The contractor went back to making sane buildings starting from the foundation upward. Clients slept soundly under the floating carpet.

And the donkeys?
Of course, continued to carry the extra load without their legs trembling.

Losing Steam

It was at the inauguration of the grand railway offices, with a 3000 capacity. G was seated in the front row, next to the current head Manager At Railway Division - let's call him MARD[1].

'I often wonder...'
The current MARD seemed to be in a confessional mood today, while G was slipping into flashback.

Four MARDs had changed position since the construction of the office started some years ago. To break the ice and delve deeper into the workings of the railways, G had curiously initiated a chat with the first of the MARDs, 'It's good. With this new division being formed, we will have more tracks and trains.'

'Noo, we are not adding any new tracks or trains or stations for that matter!' The first MARD was crystal clear.

'Are the adjoining divisions too overloaded?' G was innocent.

'No dear, everything is working fine. The British already set it up for us,' said the first MARD with surety.

'Then? Why a new division?' G continued with his innocence.

'New divisions are formed to create jobs. This will create over 20,000 new ones; the Minister seems pro-development and the country looks progressive. So, everyone is happy.'

---

1. *Man in Hindi.*

G was already perturbed by the railway's strange colonial hangover. He had come to understand that any decision above a couple of lacs[2] needed approval from the zonal office, situated far off in the Megapolis-on-an-Island. Approved or not, a junior employee carried the request letter, travelling 500 kilometres on the berth of a three-tier air-conditioned compartment of an overnight train. This entire to and fro journey would take a couple of days, during which he would stay at the official railway accommodation in the South-Megapolis-on-an-Island, one of the costliest real estates in the world. Owners of the largest land bank in the country, the railways, of course don't value it.

G also understood that the railways don't acknowledge any email, courier, post or even their own RMS[3]. They send their horsemen by train instead. No wonder people travel sleeping on newspaper laid on the floor, as their berths never get reserved.

*

'I often wonder that for days together...'
The current MARD seemed to be in a confessional mood today, while G was now immersed in flashback.

Hailing from the Hilly-Home-Town, one of the oldest railway divisions in the steamy days, G always had a link with it. His stories are all full of train episodes, more misses than catches.

Along with a train-spotting Italian friend of theirs, G and his wife, Constant K[+], had recently made a three-day trip to Morbi and Wankaner[4], to document the last running steam locomotives. This beautiful national heritage was being dismantled and sold as scrap. G even wanted to buy one of these antiques to keep in his courtyard. Just two things came in his way; there was no courtyard and he had no money.

+ *Refer to the story, 'Wet Love,' page 105*
2. *Equivalent to 100 thousand.*
3. Railway Mail Service. *The railways operated their own mail service, besides carrying mail from the* Indian Postal Service.
4. *Two towns in the Western Gujarat. The meter gauge line between them was last operated in February 2000, before steam was completely discontinued in India.*

*

'I often wonder that for days together, I have not done...'
The current MARD seemed to be in a confessional mood today, while G
sank deeper and deeper into flashback.

The railway office building was a lofty structure. All passages looked into a three-storeyed atrium space that turned out to be exactly as G had wished. Some time back, when G mentioned designing a railway building to our guru-of-all-gurus, architect Balkrishna Doshi, he said just one thing, 'They still live in the colonial era. G, it's your chance to do grand spaces!'

It was so true, realised G soon after, but added to his guru's dictum: grand spaces, spoilt by the worst of contractors!

Anyway, the building was complete, and it also received the Best Railway Building of the Year Award, given by the railways to the railways themselves.

Just one wish had remained unfulfilled - G's animal instinct! It was to photograph this 300 foot long edifice, before it turned into a typical file-pile government office. In continuation with his infatuation of shooting animals against his buildings, G had secretly desired for it to be shot alongside an elephant to go with the mammoth scale of the building. Of course, he would not find a white elephant, so his wish would have to be just black.

Shooting with elephants is an elephantine task. They are expensive, take a day to arrive and need 40 kilograms of feed while they trample all the lawns, bushes and shrubs. This is if you are lucky. If not, there is the housekeeping bill and the stink that one has to live with afterwards.

*

'I often wonder that for days together, I have not done any work whatsoever!'
The current MARD seemed to be in a confessional mood today, while G
suddenly snapped back to real time.

Aghast, he thought. Why tell Me? Why tell me Now? Now that the building was over and just a photoshoot remains? What could he reply to the confessional MARD? Many tracks crossed his mind.

Should it be with compassion?
'Yeah, that's right. I too, hardly work...'

Or should it be in praise?
'At least you realise you don't do any work; most people don't even...'

Or just be shrewd as planned?
'Can you get me an elephant...please...?'

It was then that it struck him, deep from his childhood, the loco dreams and secret motives.
'Can you get yourself a steam locomotive?'

The confessional MARD was caught off guard. He had just been given work to do. He was in a fix. If he refused, he would be the one responsible for his own guilt. If he agreed, he would not be able to confess that he didn't have work to do.

He had a busy month ahead - to locate a defunct steam engine, stop it from being turned into scrap and then bring it to the building.

He worked overtime and moved a decommissioned non-moving engine. That too, without rails. The gigantic steam engine was indeed dwarfed in front of the mammoth building. Guru-of-all-gurus, Doshi's vision was right on track.

MARD no longer seemed to be in a confessional mood, while G continued to go into slumber.

Can I Hug You?
🌶

'*Can I hug you?*'

It was the first time in the known life of G that someone proposed this to him. His pounding heart was in a dil[1]-*emma. We will attend to the hug later. Let's fast-forward a few years ahead for now.*

'They are unloading your concrete wall from the truck.' It was Client Su-Man on the phone with G.

'Who? Mine? Wall??'

'Who else would ask for a tonne of concrete?' Su-Man was sure that if it's concrete, G had to be behind it.

'Why would I? I was only to check the concrete finish at your site the day after. That's all!' G recalled.

'Oh! I told Manager Nil not to proceed without your approval. They seem to have uprooted the wall itself and brought it for you,' concluded Su-Man.

It was a case of the well having gone to the thirsty, all thanks to Su-Man's express instructions and the instant compliance by his trusted and very obedient Manager Nil, let's call him Nil-Man.

Everything around Su-Man was measured to the millimetre, timed to the nanosecond, every action and reaction micro-

---

1. *Heart in Hindi.*

managed. People around Su-Man ticked like clocks. Their minds, breaths and heartbeats would all align like grains in an hourglass. No errors, no excuses, no emotions!

Just a few days earlier, during a meeting, there had been a call from Su-Man's wife. His young son had fallen and was crying.

'*Papa, Papa*[2]...can you come fast?'

'Don't worry *beta*[3], I'm at it!'

Su-Man had instantly called the trusted Nil-Man on the intercom. 'Please take my son to a hospital and give me an update.'

'Sure, Su-Man *bhai*[4]!'

Nil-Man was very efficient. Su-Man's wife wasn't happy though.

'My top manager and my trusted doctor - they are better than anything I can do myself!' Su-Man had justified to his wife and continued with the meeting.

Introductions over, now let's time travel a few years into the past, before the impending hug. Su-Man was driving G to his newly acquired 600 acre site some 50 kilometres outside the Beloved-city-of-A-Bad. He was carrying an A4[5] size map that he had himself drawn out on his last visit; it included speed breakers with heights, potholes with depths, dhabbas[6] with menus, electric lines with light poles and culverts with their spans, all marked to the dot. This hand-drawn map from 30 years ago would beat hollow the 3-dimensional Google *map of today. Everything was happening as per the map.*

They had now reached the vast 600 acre site.

---

2. *Father in Hindi.*
3. *Son in Hindi.*
4. *Brother in Hindi.*
5. *Standard paper size of 8.3 x 11.4 inches.*
6. *Roadside eatery.*

'Last time I had climbed this light pole till the halfway mark and got a good aerial view of the site. G you are lighter than me, you sure can climb higher!' Su-Man prodded G.

In those pre-Google, pre-drone days, G had no option. Su-Man, the man provoking the very young and light G, was probably one of the most prolific forces in the industry in those days. Intelligent, ruthless and a taskmaster with a meteoric rise. Their brand was the one to watch out for.

After G's spate of winning design competitions[7] which largely remained unbuilt[+], he was picked up as an associate by the large architectural firm of a big architect, let's call him Big-Bi, where he was working on Su-Man's extremely fast-track industrial projects; so fast-track that G would be assigned only 24 hours to study, analyse, correct, improve and draw up any revisions in designs that came from specialist industry consultants.

While both G and Su-Man would start their day at 5 a.m., Su-Man would be ready on spot for tea and phone calls, while G would be cleaning his Italian coffee machine after some cryptic SMS[8] texting to the office phone from his royal-blue pot[++]. While one would give incisive instructions of the day sending shockwaves, the other doodled and yearned for a punny solution puzzling everyone. But one thing common to both was their team, who could never get the hang of them.

'Would you do a house for me?' Su-Man asked G out of the blue, one fine day.

'Sure. I'll let Big-Bi know.' G was following protocol.

'No! I want You to design it.'

+   *Refer to the story, 'Only Time Would Tell,' page 111*
++ *Refer to the story, 'A Piece of Blue Putridity,' page 65*
7.   *Architecture Design Competition, which gives architects the chance to be recognised and win public project commissions.*
8.   *Short Message Service. Before* WhatsApp *and mobile data became commonplace, a single text message allowed for only 160 characters. Exceeding this limit even by one character, meant being charged double.*

'I am an associate on only some projects of Big-Bi. He decides who heads a project.'

'Okay. I'll tell Big-Bi then.'

Big-Bi had till now only involved G in Su-Man's greenfield industrial campuses, which were away from the Beloved-city-of-A-Bad. This house for a multi-generational joint family would be part of the new 600 acre site, just outside the city, where a yet light G was climbing up the light pole. He chose the house location close to a natural pond and asked for two weeks to make a concept presentation.

The day arrived. The haze in the light was wavering, the wind outside had no direction or clue.

As G walked in for the meeting, there was flicker in the CFL[9] tube.

'What's this?' asked Su-Man. G had walked in with just some charcoal sticks[10].

'This is charcoal. We use it for drawing rough sketches.'

'Oh, you are going to draw my house live for me?'

'Yes, the fundamentals!' Thus spoke H[11], from deep inside G.

In those days, G had no money except the backing of Big-Bi. He hadn't come down the halfway mark on the light pole yet.

'Then wait! Let me call my senior managers too! They should

---

9. *Compact Fluorescent Lamp*
10. *Made by burning organic matter, the sticks produce bold black lines that create an array of rich and dark tones. It provides a great control over marks and is suitable for smudging besides sketching.*
11. *Howard Roark is the protagonist in Ayn Rand's famous book* The Fountainhead. *He is an architect who battles conventional norms and refuses to compromise with an architectural establishment unwilling to accept innovation.*

know how architects work.' He called on the intercom with undue excitement: 'Urgent. Come! G is drawing!'

Soon enough, the three managers, including the obedient Nil-Man, were surrounding G, who then asked for some paper. With Su-Man in front and the trio looking over his shoulder, G began by drawing a line across the paper.

'This is the line of worldly life!'

There was pin drop silence. Charcoal crumbs shimmered as the CFL tube flickered above. G took a breath and continued further. He now drew a vertical line crossing the earlier one.

'Now what is this?' Su-Man was curious as hell.

Nothing measured, paper rough and instruments smudgy, like a jig with a pause. The wind outside was blowing in the North-East direction now. The CFL tube stopped flickering.

'This is the line that joins the nature from inside us to the nature outside of us!'

No one spoke for a minute. After a while, Su-Man stood up. 'Can I hug you?'

It was the first time in the known life of G that someone proposed this to him. His pounding heart was in a *dil*-emma.

Su-Man came around his large executive table and hugged G with both arms. The three managers were blown. The CFL tube blew out too.

Anyway, hug over but not the story of charcoal. Stick around.

'This would make a fantastic house!' Su-Man announced with a blush and requested, 'Can I please keep this drawing with me?'

'It'll smudge. Normally we throw these away.'

Humbled H was now stuck inside smug G, balancing himself on the top of the light pole.

'I want to keep all your sketches; how do I preserve them?' Su-Man insisted.

'We normally use a fixer, but even common hairspray will do.'

'Nil-Man please do get me hairspray from a parlour nearby. I am keeping the drawing safe on my table till then.'

Perturbed, Nil-Man left the scene. Besides managing projects worth crores[12] and rushing Su-Man's son to the hospital, he was also now at a beauty parlour sampling hairspray.

Epilogue:

Later, Nil-Man and G became good friends as they worked on Su-Man's projects together. Even today, once drinks are down and conversations run dry, he never misses asking G one last question.

'What was in that crooked charcoal cross that Su-Man came and hugged you?'

G always has his counter ready. 'You tell first. Did you Really cut and send that concrete wall for Me?'

Some essential questions will always remain unanswered. Halfway through the house construction, the company went bankrupt; the two partner brothers Su-Man and Su-Man2 had split. The house was

---

12. *Each crore is equivalent to 10 million.*

abandoned, there was no joint family left. All their projects stopped abruptly and G's association with Big-Bi's firm ended as abruptly. G slid down the light pole, back to the two drawing boards in his borrowed River-by-the-Ashram studio and the birds outside[+].

I wonder even today, what had happened on that fateful day?

Seeing someone dare to distil the essence with bare hands in a blunt move, had him overwhelmed. Without any inhibition, the measured and disciplined Su-Man became a floodgate open with emotions, which even G found hard to fathom.

Wish the partner brothers had only hugged each other!

+ *Refer to the story, 'Only Time Would Tell,' page 111*

Wit •ness to Mat •Haroo (मत• हारो) Spirit

Young Priest and the Temple of Love

The first-in-line, celibate Young Priest was a man of good taste.

Not just young, he was soft-spoken, with an ear for music. He, along with his Senior Guruji had drifted into the M-Ass-Studio one day, to have their new *ashram*[1] and temple designed by us. Knowing G's simple, non-ornate and clean approach, this action was testimony enough of their broad outlook towards religion and associated paraphernalia. With no religious affiliation, G had still agreed to do it, keeping in mind what the great Masters[+], Corb-Ando-Scarpa, had achieved erecting places of worship, world over.

G has been leaving the prayer rooms to specialist mandir[2] *decorators, who deal with the clients and the Gods directly. With no methods to verify and compare costs like other building items, the faith-based temple building is blessed with money. For G, it is fine, as long as the Gods and their opulence are safely locked inside and out of view - a territory he does not normally venture into.*

With no sprawling greens or open land around, the case here was a bit different. The requirement of large floor areas on a tight urban site meant the complex had to be a multi-storeyed one. Generally, religious endeavours have good financial backing, but not here, or so we were told. It had to be on a shoestring budget with the maximum number of rooms for pilgrims, and maybe that is the reason they approached

+   *Refer to the story, 'You Don't Say NO to the Underworld,' page 1*
1.   *A hermitage, monastic community or other place of religious retreat.*
2.   *A Hindu prayer space which is usually ornamented.*

ground-bound architects like us, instead of specialist temple builders. While temple architecture is based on rules specific to each God, here the sect believed in not one but multiple Gods. Whose rules could G possibly follow?

It was a challenge as much as it was a clue. Fortunately, there was a buffer between him and the Senior Guruji in the guise of this Young Priest, so the going was smooth. G only had to give his *fundas*[3] of how open-ended the temple design was, so as not to offend any Gods placed within. He ingrained into the Young Priest the idea of natural light falling on the curved walls of the temple, which would be the only adornment, instead of religious carvings and inlay work that were expected at the very least.

The Young Priest, a graduate in philosophy, took G's thoughts to the Senior Guruji and got them sanctioned. Walking the tightrope, they managed to construct the temple as they wanted. The shadows falling on complex curved walls looked very sensuous, but the central idol was yet to be sourced. It was decided that amongst all the Gods, this would be of Lord Shiva: the creator and destroyer of the universe.

'Let's not have an idol here and just place a stone *Shivling*[4] that is symbolic of Lord Shiva,' G had slipped it slowly into the mind of the Young Priest, imagining only abstract forms in the centre.

Unknowingly, G's tryst with this suggestion was moving him closer to the destruction of his own universe. People normally don't meddle with other people's faith.

'That's a nice idea, G*ji*[5], I will discuss it with Guruji and get back to you.' The Young Priest was now motivated.

---

3. *Slang for fundamental principles or ideas in Hindi.*
4. *An abstract or aniconic representation of Lord Shiva. The* Mahabharata *and the* Puranas *relate narratives that identify the* lingam *as the phallus of Shiva. Often it rests in the centre of a lipped, disk-shaped object, the* yoni, *which is an emblem of the goddess Shakti (Source: Britannica Encyclopaedia)*
5. *Ji is a suffix used at the end of the name as a sign of respect.*

'We could get a good contemporary sculptor to make it.' Now G had crossed the thin line.

'Fine, *Gji*, wouldn't that be expensive?' said the Young Priest. The proposition had strangely gone through smoothly.

'No no! I know a few artists, for Gods they won't charge much.' G pushed further.

'Okay, let me know, *Gji*.' This too went down well.

At least within themselves, G and the Young Priest had replaced the intended idol of Lord Shiva in the Sanctum Sanctorum[6], with a *Shivling*, an abstract sculpture of male and female union to be carved by a free-spirited sculptor.

'Guruji has sanctioned, but found it a bit expensive. Instead of hiring a sculptor, why don't You make a drawing, *Gji*? We can get it enlarged in stone by our regular idol carvers.' The Young Priest seemed to want it more than even G now. It made perfect sense; this was going to be his empire in some years after the ageing Senior Guruji. It's him who would head and be remembered by the people visiting this unique temple.

'Of course, why not!' G didn't mind as long as the centre of the temple was a sculpture and not an idol.

From drawing mechanical details and banal plans in his red sketchbook, G started drawing *lingums* and *yonis*[7]. Some sketches were shown to the Young Priest.

'Yes! Yes! *Gji*, please go ahead and make a small model for us,' he said excitedly.

Under G's instructions, an intern was put on the job of turning the sketches into multiple clay models. The clay model selected

---

6. *Temple's innermost part where the image or sculpture of the deity is kept.*
7. *The male and female reproductive organs - the phallus and vulva.*

by the Young Priest was then sent to Pink-city-of-Idol-Carvers.

'Let's make it even larger; funds are not an issue. I hope your floor can take the load.' The Young Priest had taken over now and opened the coffers for the sculpture.

From the originally conceived height of 2 feet, the *Shivling* became a mammoth 5 feet high, dwarfing all the other Gods idols that were placed around it. The idol carvers were thrilled, as in their generation, they had not carved a *Shivling* so large. The Young Priest was ecstatic.

The now 8 tonne *Shivling* had to be carved out hollow from below, to reduce its weight, and yet, extra steel girders had to be erected under the temple floor, to safely carry the larger-than-life load. Two large cranes were used to lift the huge sculpture and on the most auspicious day chosen by the Senior Guruji, the *Shivling* was installed at the centre of the curvaceous space. All the other Gods stood around as mute witnesses to the grand spectacle.

G still feared backlash. Installation isn't enough. He had overheard the Young Priest talk about a milk-bath ritual by the Senior Guruji. Once bathed in milk and blessed, no changes could be made. But until then, the earth could still shake, the roof could fall and the floor could cave in. Even though he could not sit cross-legged[+], G was keeping his fingers crossed, hoping nothing would happen to his God in the meantime.

Finally, on a chosen day, the *Shivling* was bathed in pure cow milk by the Senior Guruji.

Milk bathing soothed everyone.

*

The temple opened to huge success and was being thronged with people. Senior Guruji gave sermons to much larger gatherings now. The Young Priest walked the corridors of faith and power,

---

+   *Refer to the story, 'The Old Monk Who Bought Gin-O-Logi,' page 15*

with a sense of pride and ownership. His day would also come soon.

Milk bathing soothed everyone.

*

The *Shivling* models were boxed and put on display at the M-Ass-Studio. The intern got her bachelor's degree and went back home. We mortals went back to work on our ground-bound projects. Everything went back to routine.

Milk bathing soothed everyone.

*

And then one fine day...

A video of the Young Priest went viral. He was seen announcing that under no compulsions and purely on his own free will, he was renouncing the sect and temple. He had married one of his disciples and was starting a family.

Not just the Senior Guruji, not just the crowds, not just the M-Ass-Studio, not just the Young Priest...

Milk bathing had indeed soothed everyone.

Lord Shiva: the God of creation and destruction, was at routine work too!

Wit •ness to Mat •Haroo (मत• हारो) Spirit

Moha Maya
🌶 🌶 🌶

It was live on national TV.
Breaking News!
Too difficult to break, MOHA is being blown apart.

Patrons of design come in all kinds of avatars. They may be hearty Donors[+], forgiving Dons[++] or smart Diamantaires[+++]. But N-the silent one[++++], had such rarest of rare hidden talents, that they left all the creative leaps of G put together, in sheer insignificance.

N-the silent one's house was located strategically between the land and the sea, right on the rocky beach; its thick curved walls rhyming with the other ruined forts that lined the Sea-of-Arabia. Like its inspiration, it was finished ruggedly, non-opulent and unassuming for an elite, upwardly-mobile client from the Megapolis-on-an-Island. It was aptly named MOHA, through a simple abbreviation generated out of G-System Code UNBOND700[+++++], indicating the name of client, type of building and its postal location.

MOHA was coming up slowly and steadily.

Little did anyone know then that the name *MOHA* - Hindi for attachment - actually did more than enough justice to the passionate anecdotes that followed and became one with

---

+   *Refer to the story, 'GDP and Sin-Tax,' page 131*
++   *Refer to the story, 'You Don't Say NO to the Underworld,' page 1*
+++   *Refer to the story, 'Sleepless Nights,' page 55*
++++   *Refer to the story, 'Scape Goat and the Cross-Legged Mummy,' page 151*
+++++   *Refer to the story, 'MUAH!!!' page 83*

the house. The site forces, not just geographical but even sociopolitical, were quite hostile. The crew, however, stayed on.

They were a mix of multistate mates whose names translated from Hindi, we discovered later, were also their personalities. G: *victorious master* architect; A: *highly exalted* contractor; D: *ever-joyous* interior coordinator; and M: *praise-worthy* project manager; all brought together by V: *priceless* negotiator. Added to this were countless labourers from the fertile plains of the Ganges who kept the site alive and kicking.

MOHA was meant to be a retreat for leisure. The loving act of house creation was at such a laidback pace that we could see even lethargic government works like a rural road, a mega flyover and even a remote boat jetty overtaking ours, and their construction getting completed during our endless site visits.

Reaching the site itself was no mean feat; it was like going to a faraway land in a fairy tale, and we used all possible transportation of air, water and land[+] to get there. Into this faraway land would arrive the Fiery Fairy A, restless like a butterfly, as if looking for nectar. She was the real client; her husband, N-the silent one, was just the financer.

MOHA continued to come up slowly and steadily.

True to G's fame for generating fertile ground wherever he steps, we witnessed Fiery Fairy A deliver two offspring, neither surrogates nor twins. Such was the potency of MOHA.

The site engineer was from a distant land and needed the STD. ISD.PCO[1] often. So much so that he got trapped in his own MOHA entrapment at the sight of a local village belle who ran the phone booth. They married and he settled here with his newborn.

+   *Refer to the story, 'Damsels and Dumb-bells,' page 143*
1. *Subscriber Trunk Dialling. International Subscriber Dialling. Public Call Office. From the mid to the late 90s, the yellow public telephone booths with STD.ISD. PCO written in black, were the primary source of telecommunication before the advent of pagers and mobile phones.*

The labour colony was also witness to many labour pains, and each time we could see the site bubbling with new life. With every new season, we had to befriend new puppies - even they were part of this fertility festivity. I was not spared either and was blessed with a daughter, while G also managed one son. MOHA itself didn't have a delivery date in sight.

MOHA went on to come up slowly and steadily.

Through long gestations, frequent visits, revisiting decisions and statutory approvals, everyone's lives, including some from the next generation that were born during this period, got entwined in this never-ending creation.

With enough comedy-of-errors and more than enough tragedy-of-corrections, MOHA literally became a web of frozen emotions cast in concrete and etched in stone. Everyone involved, fairies to family help, female to male, people to pets, lived a significant part of their lives at MOHA, before moving on to another time, another space, another matter.

MOHA had come up steadily and slowly.

While G kept taking creative naps, N-the silent one, was quietly making breakthroughs in his affairs of the monetary. Years after MOHA was completed, he ran out of luck. He and the Fiery Fairy A had to leave the shores for safe havens.

With N-the silent one absconding, the concrete and stone of MOHA became *MAYA* - Hindi for a mere illusion - of a place once created so passionately. As the world pushed for instant justice, MOHA the house, anchored between land and sea, became the easy scapegoat. A fixed asset that couldn't be uprooted was left behind in the hands of supreme powers. To show some pretence of retaliation, a smoke screen or *maya jaal* of sorts was fabricated with the supreme financial authority decision that MOHA be bulldozed.

With no value attached to the concepts and emotions manifested in frugal materials, it stood there completely lifeless, just waiting to be ruined. Emptied of its movable, removable and valuable assets like fixtures, furniture and art, MOHA was left abandoned like a decommissioned ship at the scrap yard.

After many failed attempts to bulldoze the house, tough MOHA had to be blown apart with dynamite. A live coverage of it ran on the national news channel. The dust settled, leaving nothing behind. N-the silent one, kept silent, society cheered, Vastu-Man[+] smiled and the crew took one last look...and moved on.

With MOHA gone and becoming MAYA, the timeless waves on the rocky beach are now the only witness to the web of indestructible stories strewn around.

+   *Refer to the story, 'Scape Goat and the Cross-Legged Mummy,' page 151*

Notes

Notes

Wit •ness to Mat •Haroo (मत• हारो) Spirit